果実酒歳時記

~季節を味わう果実酒暮らし~

Fruit wine calendar

- Enjoy Fruit Liquor Life in Seasons -

【はじめに】

ボタン一つで世界中の食材が手に入る時代ですが、自然の恵みや旬の幸はまた格別なもの。

四季折々に目にする果物や植物素材をおいしい果実酒に仕立て、季節の行事やイベントに合わせて楽しくいただこうという果実酒歳時記です。

1年が12カ月だと大雑把すぎるので、季節感のある二十四節気を目安に、クリスマスやバレンタインなど、日本に定着した行事も加えてみました。

今風二十四節気で、新しい果実酒を味わってみましょう。

果実酒は梅酒だけじゃない!と感動します。

[Introduction]

Nowadays, you can get almost all ingredients all around the world by one click, but having fresh picks or seasonal foods still brings special experience.

This fruit wine calendar contains information to make great fruit wines from fruits and other plant ingredients in season, which we recommend to enjoy at the corresponding seasonal events.

Fruit wines are introduced based on 24 solar terms instead of 12 months, which might be too rough to express seasonality precisely. Events are also included which are common in Japan today such as Christmas or Valentine's Day.

Taste new fruit wines with the modern-day arranged solar terms.

You will find your new favorite fruit wines other than Umeshu (a kind of plum liquor).

目次

【レシピ欄の記号の意味】
▼漬け込み期間
■おすすめの飲み方

[Meaning of Symbols]
"▼" provides a steeping period.
"■" introduces a recommended way of tasting.

立春

待ちに待った春の到来。

まだまだ寒さは厳しいですが、

春の兆しもそこかしこに

見え始め、陽だまりには

野花や蕗の薹が見つかることも。

旧暦では立春に近い新月の日が

元旦で新年、中国では春節です。

Rissyun　Around February 4 to 18

The long-waited spring has come.

The cold is still severe, but the signs of spring begin to appear here and there. Wild flowers and Fukinoto can be found in the sun.

In the lunar calendar, New Year's Day falls on the new moon day near Rissyun, and "Shunsetsu" in China.

バレンタインデーとチョコレート

＊聖バレンタインデーの起源は古代ローマ時代に遡るとか。兵士の婚姻を禁止したローマ皇帝に従わず、迫害の下で殉教した聖ヴァレンティヌスが処刑された日で、恋人たちが愛を誓う日に。

＊バレンタインデーにチョコレートを贈る習慣は19世紀後半のイギリスから。日本では神戸の製菓会社の広告掲載が最初といわれ、1970年代後半から日本型バレンタインデーが広まったようです。

Valentine's Day and Chocolate

*The origin of Valentine's Day is said to trace back to the ancient Roman era. It is the day in which Saint Valentinus, who didn't obey the order of the Roman emperor that banned soldiers from marriage, was executed. Nowadays, couples bow their love each other on this day.

*The custom to present chocolate on Valentine's Day started in the late 19th century in England.

山菜のトップバッターが蕗の薹。凍てつく大地を割って芽吹く姿は、力強さと愛おしさを感じます。ほろ苦い風味と深い香りは味噌との相性がいいので蕗味噌に。天麩羅でもほどよく香りが残ります。

Fukinotou　*Petasites japonica*

Fukinotou is the king of the wild vegetables. The figure of Fukinotou breaking the frozen earth and sprouting is powerful and lovely.The bitter taste and deep aroma go well with miso, so it makes delicious Fukimiso (蕗味噌).The fragrance remains well even in tempura.

フキノトウ酒　Fukinotou Liquor

～深山碧が美しい早春のほろ苦香り酒～
A scented bitter sweet liquor of early spring, with a color of beautiful deep green -

＊フキノトウ……………………………… 中くらいのもの５個
Fukinotou　Medium-size 5 pieces

＊35度ホワイトリカー ……………………………… 500ml
35% white liquor

＊蕗の薹は半分に切る。沸騰したお湯で10〜20秒ほど湯がき、冷水で冷やして水気を絞る。
Cut the Fukinotous in half.In boiling water, wash them for about 10-20 seconds, cool in water, and squeeze them lightly to remove the moisture.

▼３日〜１週間。3 days to 1 week.
■お湯割り・ロック。和風料理に。With hot water, or on the rocks.Suitable for Japanese cuisine.

★蕗の薹はなるべく開いていない固いものがよいでしょう。
★It is better to use hard ones that don't open so much.

【オレンジ＆ココア】

スイートオレンジではバレンシアとネーブルが有名。日本でもさまざまな品種が開発されています。ココアは、カカオ豆を発酵・焙煎・除皮・磨り潰し・一部脱脂・粉砕したもの。カフェイン類のテオブロミンも。

Orange and Cocoa
Citrus sinensis & Theobroma cacao

Valencia and Navel are famous brands of sweet oranges.Various varieties have been developed in Japan as well.Cocoa is made from cacao beans which are fermented, roasted, peeled, ground, partially defatted, and crushed.It also contains caffeine theobromine.

オレンジココア酒　Orange Cocoa Liquor

〜甘美な恋のリキュール〜
- A liqueur of sweet love -

＊国産オレンジ……2個分の皮
Japanese orange　2whole peels
＊純ココア……………… 25 g
Pure cocoa
＊氷砂糖……………… 70 g
Rock sugar
＊25度甲類焼酎 …… 720ml
25% korui shochu

＊国産オレンジは皮を洗って水気をふき取り、白いワタがつかないよう、皮を削ぐようにむきます。
For Japanese oranges, wash the skins and wipe off, and shave the skins off being careful not to allow the white stuffs to attach.

▼1週間。 1 week.
■牛乳割り、ロック。 With milk or on the rocks.

★濾す時のポイントは、ココアを沈殿させたまま静かに傾けること。
★A tip for filtering is to tilt the container gently with cocoa precipitated.
★輸入柑橘類は、防カビ剤が付いているので皮は使えません。
★Fungicide is attached on foreign citrus fruits, so cannot be used.

雨水 二月十九日〜三月四日頃

降る雪が雨に変わり、
積雪を解かして大地を潤す時候が雨水。
枯れ野にも緑が目立ちはじめ、
梅花香ただよう中、
観梅も真っ盛り。
農家でも田畑の準備が始まり、
時候の終わりには
雛祭りも待っています。

Usui   Around February 19 to March 4

Usui is the season when the falling snow turns into rain, melting the snow on the ground, and wetting.

Green also appears in the withered fields. People are enjoying seeing plum flowers in the plum-scented air.

Farmers are preparing for the fields, and at the end of the season Hinamatsuri is waiting.

桃の節句

*桃の節句は、旧暦なら3月下旬から4月初旬で、ちょうど桃の花が満開の頃。元々は川で禊をしたり、人形に穢れを移して流したもの。江戸時代以降、雛人形を飾る女子の節句・雛祭りに定着しました。

*白酒と甘酒
白酒は酒や味醂にもち米や米麹を仕込んで1カ月程熟成させたもので、アルコールは9％前後。
甘酒はご飯やお粥に米麹を混ぜ、ひと晩保温して糖化させたもの。アルコールは含みません。

Momo no sekku or the Peach Festival

*Momo no sekku falls on late March to early April in the old calendar, in which peach flowers are in full bloom.Originally, people had a purification ceremony in a river or put their impurities to dolls which were then sent down a river. Since the Edo period, the event has been celebrated as Hinamatsuri or the Girl's Day in which people display Hinaningyo or a set of ornamental dolls.

White sake and Amazake

*White sake is made from sake and mirin with glutinous rice and rice koji, which are aged for a month. Alcohol content by volume is about 9%.
Amazake is made from rice or rice porridge with rice koji being mixed, which is then kept warm over a night for saccharification.It does not contain alcohol.

【梅花】

古い時代に中国から渡って来た梅は日本人に広く愛され、平安時代に花見といえば観梅をさしました。園芸品種が多く、地植えのほか盆栽の愛好家も。果樹としても栽培が盛んで、梅干しは日本食の代表。

Plum flower *Prunus mume*

Plums that came from China in the old days have been loved by Japanese people, and in the Heian period, people used to refer to Hanami as seeing plum blossoms.There are many horticultural varieties, including for bonsai plants not only for planting in the ground. Cultivation is thriving as a fruit tree, for making Umeboshi, one of the representative Japanese foods.

梅花酒 Plum blossom Liquor

～高貴な梅花香ただよう早春酒～
- An early-spring liquor with noble fragrance of plum blossom -

＊梅花‥‥‥‥‥‥‥‥‥‥‥‥‥‥‥‥ ビンいっぱい
Plum blossom   Full of the bottle
＊25度甲類焼酎 ‥‥‥‥‥‥‥‥‥‥‥ 梅花がかぶるくらい
25%korui shochu   For quantity that covers the plum blossoms.
＊梅花はきれいな環境のものを選び、早朝に咲いて間もない花を摘んで洗わずに用います。
Select plum trees planted in a clean environment and pick up the blossoms that blossomed early in the morning. Washing is not needed.

▼3日。3 days.
■ロック、梅酒ブレンド。紅茶にも。On the rocks, or in blend with Umeshu.Also suitable for tea.

【苺】

イチゴの正式名はオランダイチゴで、日本には江戸時代にオランダから入り、本格栽培は明治以降。ハウス栽培が主流でいちご狩りも盛んに行われ、これからが旬。品種改良も盛んな人気フルーツです。

Strawberry *Fragaria chiloensis*

Strawberries are formally called "Fragaria", which were imported from Netherland to Japan in the Edo period of which cultivation started from the Meiji period at full scale.They are mainly cultivated in greenhouses offering strawberry picking, which is popular in Japan. Their season starts in this season. Strawberry is a popular fruit with a lot of improvements actively done so far.

いちご酒 Strawberry Liquor

～雛祭りにピッタリの赤い甘美な芳香酒～
- A red-colored, sweet aromatic liquor that is best for Hinamatsuri-

*イチゴ……………300ｇ　*氷砂糖…………… 50ｇ
Strawberry　　　　　　　　　　Rock sugar
*35度ホワイトリカー …………………………… 600ml
35%white liquor
*イチゴはヘタを取り、ざっと洗って水気を切る。
Hull the strawberries and wash lightly and drain.

▼3日〜1週間。 3 days - 1 week
■ロック、ソーダ割り。女性向けのお姫様酒。On the rocks or with soda.A princess liquor for women.

★酸味の欲しい方はレモンの果肉をスライスして加えます。半分〜1個分。
★If you want some sour taste, slice a lemon pulp and add it.

啓蟄

三月五日〜十九日頃

土の中で冬ごもりしていた虫たちが、
目を覚まして這い出てくるという時候。
菜の花やタンポポの
黄色い花が目立ち、
大地の歓喜を感じます。
野山や田畑、河川の土手に
春を探しに出かけましょう。

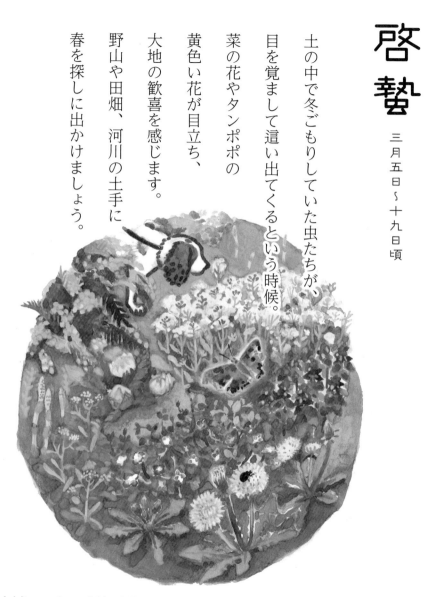

Keichitsu　Around March 5 to 19

Keichitsu is the season in which hibernating insects wake up and come out on the ground.
With canola flowers or dandelions distinctive in yellow starting to bloom here and there, you feel the delights of the spring.
Visit a mountain, field or river bank to feel the arrival of spring.

晩柑類

＊柑橘類のうち、ほぼ2月以降から店頭に並ぶ晩生のものを総称して晩柑類といいます。ミカンより大型で酸味や芳香が特徴的。収穫していったん保存熟成してから出荷されます。

＊伊予柑、八朔、甘夏（夏みかん）、日向夏、デコポン、清見タンゴール、大きいものでは文旦（ザボン）や晩白柚（バンペイユ）も。

Bankan

*Among citrus fruits, those of late ripening and in season from February are generally called "Bankan". They are larger than tangerines in size and have a characteristic sour taste and aroma. After picked, they are stored for aging for a certain period before shipped.

*Iyokan, Hassaku, Amanatsu (Natsumikan), Hyuganatsu, Dekopon, Kiyomi Tangor, and larger ones including Zabon and Banpeiyu.

【タンポポ】

日本だけでも数十種類ある　タンポポですが、よく見かけるのは四季咲きの西洋タンポポで明治期に札幌農学校が野菜として導入したもの。英語名のダンデリオンはライオンの歯、日本名は鼓に由来する。

Dandelion　*Taraxacum spp.*

There are dozens of dandelion varieties in Japan alone, but the most commonly seen are the four-season Western dandelions introduced by Sapporo Agricultural College as vegetable in the Meiji period.The English name "dandelion" comes from lion's teeth, and the Japanese name from a drum.

タンポポ酒　Dandelion Liquor

～黄色い妖精は春の薬膳酒～
- A medicinal liquor in spring, the yellow fairies -

＊タンポポ全草……………………………………………60 g
　Whole grasses of dandelion
＊35度ホワイトリカー …………………………………720ml
　35% white liquor
＊花の咲いているタンポポを根ごと掘りあげ、泥をよく落として水洗いし、根は小口切り、葉や花はそのままで水気をきる。
　Dig up dandelions in bloom with its roots and wash them thoroughly to remove mud. Drain the leaves and flowers and cut the roots into small pieces

▼ 1ヶ月。1 month.
■水割り、お湯割り、ロック。With water or hot-water, or on the rocks.

★西洋タンポポは若葉をサラダなどで食べ、根は干して焙煎しお茶（タンポポコーヒー）にします。★漢方では根を蒲公英（ホコウエイ）と呼び、清熱・解毒・利尿の作用が知られます。
★For western dandelions, you can enjoy their young leaves in salads, dry and roast roots to make tea (or dandelion coffee).★In Kampo, the root is called Hokouei(蒲公英), and its effects of antipyretic, detoxification, and diuresis are known.

【甘夏】

甘夏は、初夏が旬の夏みかんより甘みがあり春が旬。夏みかんの枝変わり品種で、正式名は川野夏橙（カワノナツダイダイ）といい、昭和になってから育成されました。皮はマーマレードや砂糖菓子にも加工されます。

Amanatsu *Citrus natsudaidai*

Amanatsu is in season in spring and sweeter than Natsumikan (in season in early summer). It is a variety of Natsumikan, derived from a bud sport, with its official name "Kawano Natsu Daidai, which has been cultivated since the Showa period.Their peels are also processed into marmalade and suger orange peels.

甘夏酒 Amanatsu Liquor

～ほんのりビターな柑橘焼酎～
- A citrus shochu with slight bitterness -

＊甘夏 ·· 1個分の皮
　　Amanatsu　　　　　　　　　　　　　　　　　1whole peel
＊25度甲類焼酎 ··· 720ml
　　25% korui shochu
＊甘夏はお湯で皮を洗い、白いワタをよけて皮をむきます。
　　Wash with hot water and peel the amanatsu removing its white parts

▼1週間。1 week.
■水割り、お湯割り。With water or hot-water.

★果肉も一緒に漬ける場合は房から出し、むいた皮と氷砂糖を加え35度ホワイトリカーで漬けます。皮は1週間であげ、1ヶ月熟成させて濾します。甘酸っぱい女性向けの美酒に。
★If you want to steep the pulp together, take it out of the bunch to steep in 35% white liquor with the peels and rock sugar. Take the peels after a week and age the liquor for a month and filter it. A sweet, sour taste sake is ready for women.

春分

三月二十日～四月三日頃

冬至翌日から延び始めた昼の長さが、
ようやく夜と同じになる日が春分。
春分を挟んで
前後3日の1週間は、
ご先祖様を供養する春彼岸。
後半は別れと出会いの季節、
そして桜前線も上昇してきます。

Shunbun [Spring Equinox]   Around March 20 to April 3

The spring equinox is the day when the length of the day that began to extend from the next day of the winter solstice finally becomes equal to the night.

The week crossing the spring equinox at its middle is Haruhigan, a period observed to pay respects to ancestors.

The second half is the season with a series of meetings and farewells, and the cherry blossom front is also advancing.

イースター（復活祭）

＊キリスト教国では、春分の日の後の満月の最初の日曜日は重要な祭日イースター（復活祭）。キリストの復活を祝う移動祝日で、年や宗派で異なります。

＊イースターに付き物なのがイースターエッグ（復活祭の卵）とイースターバニー（復活祭のウサギ）。彩色・装飾されたゆで卵は、死と復活の象徴。卵を運んでくるウサギは、多産なので豊穣の象徴という。

Easter[Resurrection Sunday]

*In Christian countries, Easter, an important feast, falls on the first Sunday following the full moon after the Vernal Equinox.The days of this moveable feast to celebrate the resurrection of Christ varies according to year and sect.

*The typical accompaniments of Easter are Easter eggs and Easter bunnies.Colored and decorated boiled eggs are a symbol of death and resurrection.Rabbits that carry eggs are said to be a symbol of fertility since they are so prolific.

Celery *Apium graveolens*

Celery is a medicinal herb used for intestines, tonics and amulets during the ancient Greek and Roman eras. It was introduced to Japan during the Azuchi-Momoyama period and was also called Kiyomasa Ginseng or Dutch Mitsuba. It became popular as a flavored vegetable after World War II.

【セロリ】

セロリは、古代ギリシャ・ローマ時代には整腸・強壮剤や魔除けに用いられた薬草で、日本には安土桃山時代に渡来し、清正人参やオランダミツバとも呼ばれました。香味野菜として普及したのは戦後から。

セロリ酒　Celery Liquor

〜スッキリした春の野菜酒〜
- A refreshing, spring vegetable liquor -

＊セロリ‥‥‥‥‥‥‥‥‥‥150ｇ　＊レモン果肉‥‥‥‥‥　1個分
　Celery　　　　　　　　　　　　　　　Lemon pulp　　　　For 1 piece
＊35度ホワイトリカー ‥‥‥‥‥‥‥‥‥‥‥‥‥‥‥‥ 600ml
　35% white liquor
＊セロリは5㎜くらいに斜め切りにし、レモンは皮を厚めにむいて果肉だけスライスします。
　Cut the celery diagonally to about 5 mm each, peel the lemon thickly and slice the pulp only.

▼2週間。2 weeks.
■水割り、ロック。食前酒に。With water or on the rocks.Serve as an aperitif.

★セロリは、不安定な心身のバランスを整える作用があります。
★Celery has an effect of balancing the unstable body and mind.

18

【パッションフルーツ】

キリストの受難（パッション）を名に持つ果物。日本名の果物時計草は花形が時計の文字盤に似ているところから。中南米原産で華やかな芳香が特長、丸い殻の中にゼリー状の果肉と種が詰まっています。

Passion fruit *Passiflora edulis*

A fruit having the name that means the "Passion of Christ".Its Japanese name "fruit clock grass" comes from its flower-like shape which resembles a clock face.Originating in Central and South America, it features a gorgeous fragrance and its round shell is packed with jelly-like pulp and seeds.

パッションフルーツ酒　Passion fruit Liquor

～五指に入る南国の芳香酒～
- an aromatic liquor from the south ranked in the top five -

＊パッションフルーツ……4個　＊氷砂糖………………… 50g
　Passion fruit　　　　　4 pieces　　Rock sugar

＊35度ホワイトリカー ………………………………… 600ml
　35% white liquor

＊パッションフルーツは横半分に切ります。
　Cut the passion fruit horizontally in half.

▼2週間。2weeks.
■ロック、炭酸割り。On the rocks or with soda.

★16世紀、中南米に派遣されたイエズス会の宣教師が、この花はキリストの受難を象徴している「十字架上の花」として、布教に利用したことに由来。

★この時期は、南半球からの輸入品を使いましょう。

★This flower originated from the use by a Jesuit missionary dispatched to Central and South America in the 16th century as a "flower on the cross" symbolizing the Passion of Christ.

★For this season, use imported passion fruit from the Southern Hemisphere.

清明

四月四日〜十九日頃

大地のすべてが清々しく生き生きとする季節。

花々が咲き乱れ、

桜も染井吉野から

山桜・牡丹桜、

さらに上溝桜に。

4月8日の花祭り（灌仏会）は

お釈迦様の生まれた日で、

甘露の雨が降ったとか。

Seimei   Around April 4 to 19

The season when all of the earth is refreshed and alive.

Flowers bloom, needless to say, so do cherries, which blossom one after another from Somei Yoshino to Yamazakura, Botanzakura, to Uwamizuzakura.

April 8th, in which the Flower Festival (Kanbutsue) is held, is the day when Buddha was born and it is said people had a rain of Kanro.

桜いろいろ

＊桜は日本を象徴する花だけにさまざまな品種が作られ、300～600種があると言われます。よく目にする桜をいくつか拾ってみました。

寒緋桜‥濃桃色の早咲き・開花は3月上旬

染井吉野‥お花見の代表品種・3月下旬

山桜‥白い花と赤い若葉が同時で、吉野山の桜はこれ・4月

鬱金桜‥淡い黄緑の八重咲・4月中旬

枝垂桜‥枝が垂れる桜の総称・4月

＊開花期は関東標準

Other various cherry blossoms

It is said that there are 300-600 kinds of cherry blossoms as a flower that symbolizes Japan.We picked up some of the most common cherry blossoms.

Kanhizakura: Deep pink-colored and early blossoming in late March

Somei Yoshino: Often refered to as a representative variety of Hanami, blossoming in late March

Yamazakura: White blossoms blossom and young red leaves sprout at the same time. It is the cherry blossom seen at Mount Yoshino, blossoming in April.

Ukonzakura: A pale yellow-green double cherry, blossoming in mid-April

Shidarezakura: A general term for cherry trees of which branches droop, blossoming in April.

*The blossoming period is according to the Kanto standard.

【八重桜】 八重咲きのサクラの総称

お花見桜が散って八重桜(里桜)が咲き出します。牡丹桜とも呼ばれ、ヤマザクラやオオシマザクラから八重に変化した品種の総称。お祝いの席で出される桜湯は、この花の塩漬けにお湯を注いだもの。

Yaezakura

A generic term for double cherry blossoms

After cherry petals for Hanami fall, Yaezakura (or Satozakura) starts blossoming.It is a general term for varieties of which changed to double cherries from Yamazakura and Oshimazakura, also called "Botanzakura (or peony cherry)". Sakurayu, which is served at a festive seat, is made by pouring hot water into salted blossoms.

八重桜酒　Yaezakura Liquor

〜桜特有の桜餅香が素晴らしい花酒〜
- A liquor with a wonderful sakuramochi aroma unique to cherries -

＊八重桜花……………………………… 漬け込みビンほぼ満杯
　Yaezakura petals　　　　　　　　　　　　Full of the steeping bottle
＊35度ホワイトリカー ……………… 花がひたひたになる量
　35% white liquor　　　　　　　　　　　Quantity that covers the petals.
＊花は開き始めのものを早朝に採取し、水に浸すようにしてさっと洗い、水気をきります。
　Pick up blossoms that start to open early in the morning, wash in water lightly like you soak them and drain.

▼5日以内。Within 5 days.
■ロック、ブレンド。パーティーや祝宴にも。On the rocks or in blend.For parties and banquets as well.

★八重桜酒をお菓子やゼリー・飲み物の風味付けに生かして。
★Use the Yaezakura liquor for flavoring sweets, jelly or drinks.

【ウワミズザクラ】

ウワミズザクラは上溝桜が訛ったもので、古代の亀甲占いが由来とか。白い小花が房状に咲く独特の桜で、新潟県では硬い緑の蕾を塩漬けした杏仁香（アンニンゴ）を香食します。熟果も果実酒に最適。

Uwamizuzakura *Prunus grayana*

The Uwamizuzakura is a collapse of Uwami "zo"zakura, said to be originated from ancient turtle fortune-telling.
A unique cherry blossom with white small petals blossoming in tufts. In Niigata Prefecture, its hard green buds are salted to make "Anningo", which is offered to the deceased.
Ripe fruits are also ideal for fruit wine.

ウワミズザクラ花酒　Uwamizuzakura blossom Liquor

～桜と杏仁の香りの深山花酒～
- Miyama Blossom Liquor with the scent of cherry blossoms and apricots -

＊ウワミズザクラ花蕾 ··· ビンいっぱい
　Buds of Uwamizuzakura　　　　　　　　　　　　Full of the bottle
＊35度ホワイトリカー ······································· ひたひた
　35% white liquor　　　　　　　The amount that covers the buds
＊氷砂糖 ······················· 入れないか、酒量の1/10 ～ 1/20 g
　Rock sugar　　　Go without or 1/10 - 1 / 20 grams of the liquor quantity
＊房ごと水に浸す程度に洗って水気をきる。
　Almost soak and wash the bunch in water and drain.

> ▼半月〜１カ月以内。Within half a month to 1 month.
> ■ロック、ブレンド。On the rocks or in blend.

★7〜8月に赤黒く熟す果実は、チェリーブランデーをしのぐ素晴らしい果実酒に結晶します。
★Fruits that ripen red and black in July to August make a wonderful fruit wine that are more wonderful than cherry brandy.

穀雨

穀物の発芽や生育に必要な
水分を恵む慈雨の季節、
山菜も次々と芽を出します。
しとしと降る春雨は菜種つゆとも。
「夏も近づく八十八夜」で
新茶も香り、
果物売り場には夏を先取りで
南国果実も並びます。

Kokuu　Around April 20 to May 4

The season of blessing rain that supplies water necessary for grains to germinate and grow. Wild vegetables also sprout one after another.

The spring rain that drizzles is also called "Natane (canola seed) Tsuyu (rain)".

The first-picked tea leaves are fragrant at "Eighty-eight nights when summer approaches", and tropical fruits are lined ahead of summer at fruit shops.

ウコギ科山菜

＊ヤマウドと同じウコギ科には、山菜の王様・タラの芽、ウコギ、コシアブラなども。ウコギ科はエゾウコギ（刺五加）やオタネニンジン（薬用人参）・トチバニンジン（竹節人参）など薬用植物の宝庫で、元気効果も望める春山の恵みです。

Araliaceae wild plants

In the same family as Yamado, there is also the king of wild plants, tara-no-me, and ukogi and kosiabra.The araliaceae provides a lot of medicinal plants such as Ezoukogi, Otaneninjin (a kind of ginsengs), Tochibaninjin, blessings of the spring mountain that give you energy.

【山独活】

ヤマウドは元々野生種で山菜の一種ですが、現在は栽培されています。白く長いウドは軟白栽培されたもので植物は同じ。ウドは根茎が和独活（ワドッカツ）という生薬で、身体を温め、痛みを止める効果も。

Yamaudo *Aralia cordata*

Yamaudo is originally a wild species and a kind of mountain vegetable, but is now cultivated. The white long udo is cultivated by blanching method and the species is the same. Udo is a herbal medicine with a rhizome called Waddokatsu, which has the effects of warming the body and stopping pain.

ヤマウド酒　Yamaudo Liquor

～大地の息吹を感じる爽やかな山菜酒～
- A refreshing liquor made of a wild vegetable that makes you feel the breath of the earth -

＊ヤマウド……………………………………… 300ｇ
　Yamaudo
＊35度ホワイトリカー …………………………… 600ml
　35% white liquor
＊茎を5mmほどにスライスし、葉も適当に切って使う。
　Slice the stem to about 5 mm and cut the leaves in modest sizes.

▼1ヶ月。1 month.
■ロック、水割り、お湯割り。On the rocks, or with water or hot-water

★秋にヤマウドの根茎を掘り上げて漬けてもよい。根茎には発汗・解熱・鎮痛作用が知られます。
★You can dig up Yamaudo rhizomes in autumn and steep them.The rhizomes are known for sweating, antipyretic and analgesic effects.

【マンゴー】

マンゴーは世界中の熱帯で数百の栽培品種があり、インドでは4000年以上前から栽培され、仏教経典にも登場する聖なる樹。果皮が赤く丸みのあるアップルマンゴーや、果皮が黄色で扁平なペリカンマンゴーが有名。

Mango *Mangifera indica*

Mangos have hundreds of cultivars in the tropics around the world. It has been cultivated in India for over 4000 years and mango trees are sacred and also appear in Buddhist scriptures.Red, round apple mangos and yellow, flat pelican mangos are famous.

マンゴー酒 Mango Liquor

～甘美で華やかなトロピカル果実酒～
- Sweet and gorgeous tropical fruit wine -

＊マンゴー·················· 1個　＊レモン果肉········· 1/2個分
　Mango　　　　　　 1 piece 　Lemon pulp　　　 A half

＊氷砂糖··· 40g
　Rock sugar

＊35度ホワイトリカー ······································ 600ml
　35% white liquor

＊マンゴーは皮をむき、果肉をそぎ切りにする。レモンは皮を厚めにむき、果肉をスライスする。
　Peel the mangos and shave the pulp.Peel the lemon thickly and slice the pulp.

▼2週間～1ヶ月。2 weeks to 1 month.
■ロック、炭酸割り。アイスクリームにも。On the rocks or with soda.Also suitable for ice cream.

★マンゴーはウルシ科の植物なので、皮膚の敏感な方は注意して。
★日本にはメキシコやフィリピン・タイなどから輸入されます。
★A mango is a plant of anacardiaceae, so be careful if you have a sensitive skin.
★Imported from Mexico, Philippines, Thailand, etc. to Japan.

立夏 五月五日〜二十日頃

瑞々しい新緑が輝き、
鯉のぼりが青空を泳ぐ
清々しい初夏の始まりです。
子供の日は端午の節句で
菖蒲の節句、
第二日曜日には母の日も。
花の催事も真っ盛りで、
棚田では田植えも始まります。

Rikka   Around May 5 to 20

It is the beginning of a refreshing early summer when fresh greenery shines and Koinoboris are flown in the blue sky.
Children's Day falls on Tango-no-Sekku or Shobu-no-Sekku, and Mother's Day also on the second Sunday.
Many flower events are also held and rice planting started in rice terraces.

「薬刈」（クスリガリ）とシソ科ハーブ

＊端午の節句は5月の最初の午の日という意味で、奈良・平安時代には、野山へ菖蒲や蓬などの薬草や鹿の袋角を採りに行く『薬刈クスリガリ』の習慣があったそう。

＊すっかり日本に定着した西洋ハーブはこれからが花の季節。特に調理用としてなじみのあるシソ科のハーブ類も、新芽がのびて摘み頃。フレッシュハーブを薬刈し、身近な料理で楽しもう。

＊主なシソ科のハーブには、タイム、セージ、ミント類、オレガノ、マジョラム、ローズマリーなど。バジルはちょっと早いかな？

Kusurigari and Lamiaceae herbs

*Tango-no-Sekku means the first day of May, and in the Nara and Heian periods, it is said there was a custom of "Kusurigari" to go to wild mountains to pick up medicinal herbs such as shobu and yomogi, and deer horns.

*The western herbs, which have become popular in Japan, start to bloom in this season. Lamiaceae herbs, especially familiar in cooking, are also picked when new shoots grow. Let's pick up fresh herbs and enjoy them in everyday dishes.

*Major lamiaceae herbs include thyme, sage, mint groups, oreganos, marjoram, and rosemary.Do we have to wait a little bit for basil?

【蓬】（ヨモギ）

早春に萌えたての新葉を摘んで草餅（蓬餅）をつくった蓬も、すっかり成長して大きな葉を広げています。葉は生薬：艾葉（ガイヨウ）と呼ばれ、冷えからくる不調に用いられます。特に女性にはありがたい野草。

Yomogi *Artemisia princeps*

Yomogi, of which freshly sprouted leaves are picked In early spring to make Kusamochi (or Yomogimochi), has grown completely and spreads large leaves.The leaves are a herbal medicine: they are called "Gaiyo" and is used to heal an irregular condition that comes from the cold.A wild grass that is especially appreciated by women.

ヨモギ酒　Yomogi Liquor

〜身近な野草の健康酒〜
- A healthy liquor made of a common wild grass -

＊蓬の生葉‥‥‥‥‥‥‥‥‥‥‥‥‥‥‥‥‥‥‥‥ 40ｇ
  Raw leaves of yomogi
＊35度ホワイトリカー ‥‥‥‥‥‥‥‥‥‥‥‥ 720ml
  35% white liquor
＊葉は水洗いしたのち、水気をきる程度に乾かします。
  After washing the leaves with water, drain and dry them.

▼１ヶ月以内。Within 1 month.
■ロック、お湯割り。On the rocks or with hot water.

★残った葉は、干してかるく焙煎し蓬茶に。野草茶とブレンドも。
★The remaining leaves can be dried and roasted lightly to make yomogi tea.Also can be blended with wild grass tea.

【タイム】 立麝香草 (タチジャコウソウ)

タイムはシソ科の小さな灌木で、調理用ハーブとして魚料理などに多用されます。爽やかな芳香で、古代ギリシャ・ローマ時代に「彼はタイムの香りがする」といえば青年への最高の褒め言葉でした。

Thyme *Thymus vulgaris*

Thyme is a small shrub of lamiaceae, and is often used in fish dishes as a herb for cooking. It has a refreshing fragrance, and it was the best compliment for a young man to say "he smells of thyme" in ancient Greece and Rome.

タイムワイン Thyme Wine

～胃腸にやさしい薬味ワイン～
- A medical wine good for the stomach and intestines -

＊生タイム…………………………………… 10cmの枝×5本くらい
Raw thyme　　　　　　　　　　　　　　　About five 10cm branches

＊氷砂糖……………… 50g　＊赤ワイン………… 360ml
Rock sugar　　　　　　　　　　Red wine

＊35度ホワイトリカー ………………………………… 360ml
35% white liquor

＊タイムは枝付きのまま使います。
Use thyme with branches.

▼1週間。1 week.
■ストレート、ロック、炭酸割り。食前酒に。Straight, on the rocks, or with soda.For an aperitif.

★ワインを使った果実酒は早めに飲みきりましょう。
★Drink all fruit wine that uses wine as soon as possible.

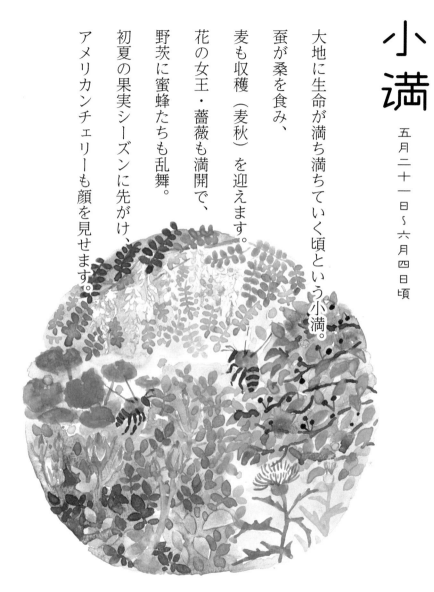

小満

大地に生命が満ち満ちていく頃という小満。

蚕が桑を食み、

麦も収穫（麦秋）を迎えます。

花の女王・薔薇も満開で、

野茨に蜜蜂たちも乱舞。

初夏の果実シーズンに先がけ、

アメリカンチェリーも顔を見せます。

Shouman　Around May 21 to June 4

Shoman is a season when life starts to fill the earth.

Silkworms eat mulberries and wheat is also harvested(Bakusyu).

The queens of flowers, roses are also in full bloom, and bees dance wildly around the thorns.

Prior to the early summer fruit season, american cherries also appear.

花のお酒

＊花のお酒は芳香や効能が主体、今からおすすめの花酒4品。

ジャーマンカモミール‥青りんごを想わせる香りで、安眠を誘う。

クチナシ‥甘い香りのお酒に。果実は着色や薬用にも。

スイカズラ‥漢方では金銀花。余分な熱を除いて血をきれいに。

紅花‥暗橙黄色で、女性にやさしい薬膳酒。原酒に半量紹興酒も。

Flower liquor

*Flower liquor mainly features its fragrance and effects, with four recommended varieties for this season.

German Chamomile: A scent reminiscent of a green apple that invites you to sleep.

Gardenia: For sweet scented sake.Fruits can be used for coloring and medicinal purposes.

Honeysuckle: Called "Kinginka (金銀花)" meaning "gold and silver flowers" in Kampo.They clean blood by removing excess heat.

Safflower: A dark orange-yellow, medicinal liquor that has effects comfortable for women.Also, try to add the half amount of Shaoxing wine to the base liquor.

Rose *Rosa genus*

Roses are one of the most loved flowers in the world, and there are a lot of horticultural varieties. They are cultivated not only for ornamental purposes but also for fragrances, foods and medicines.For flower liquor, strong fragrant varieties are suitable, and perfume roses and rosa rugosa are also recommended.

【薔薇】

薔薇は世界で最も愛される花の一つで、園芸品種も極めて多く、観賞用のほか、香料用・食用・薬用にも栽培されます。花酒用には香りの強い品種が合い、香水バラやハマナスもおすすめ。

ローズワイン　Rose Wine

〜優雅なバラ香のストレス解消ワイン〜
- An elegant rose-scented stress-relieving wine -

＊ハーブティー用の乾燥バラ………………………… 10 〜 20 g
Dried roses for herbal tea

＊氷砂糖……………… 40 g　＊赤ワイン………… 360ml
Rock sugar　　　　　　　　　　Red wine

＊35度ホワイトリカー… ………………………………… 360ml
White liquor

＊市販の乾燥バラはそのまま使用。生の場合は無農薬の花蕾を40g。
Use commercially available dried roses.When using raw ones, prepare 40g of pesticide-free flower buds.

▼3 〜 5日。3 - 5 days.
■ロック、ストレート、炭酸割り。気分転換に。On the rocks, straight, or with soda.Drink to change mood.

★乾燥バラは、ハーブショップやハーブティーコーナーで入手。
★Dried roses are available at herbal shops or herbal tea corners.

【アメリカンチェリー】

5月下旬になると、黒赤紫で大粒のサクランボが店頭に並び始めます。日本の繊細なサクランボに比べると甘味や色が濃く、価格的にもお手頃なアメリカンチェリー。果実酒には日本産より向いています。

American Cherry　*Prunus avium*

At the end of May, black, red and purple large cherries begin to line up at the store.Compared with delicate Japanese cherries, American cherries are sweeter and darker in color, and also more affordable.They are more suitable for fruit wine than Japanese cherries.

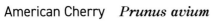

アメリカンチェリー酒　American Cherry Liquor

〜お手軽チェリーブランデー〜
- Simple cherry brandy -

* ＊アメリカンチェリー……………………………… 300 g
  American cherry
* ＊レモン果肉……… 1/2個分　＊氷砂糖……………… 50 g
  Lemon pulp　　　A half　　　Rock sugar
* ＊35度ホワイトリカー ……………………………… 600ml
  35% white liquor
* ＊チェリーは、皮に数カ所切れ込みを入れます。レモンは皮を厚めにむいて、果肉だけスライス。
  Make several cuts in the cherry skins.Peel the lemon thickly and slice the pulp only.

> ▼1ヶ月。 1 month.
> ■ロック、炭酸割り。On the rocks, or with soda.

★6月中旬になると染井吉野や山桜の実が黒く熟し、これを漬けると素晴らしいチェリー酒に結晶します。分量はアメリカンチェリーの半分を目安に。
★In mid-June, the cherries of Someiyoshino and Yamazakura become black and ripen, and they make a wonderful cherry liquor when steeped.

芒種 六月五日〜二十日頃

イネ科植物の穂先にあるトゲを
芒（ノギ）といい、
芒種はその種をまく頃。
梅雨前線が日本列島に上昇し、
田んぼの水面をわたる風が
早苗をくすぐります。
入梅とともに梅の実の収穫も始まり、
初夏の果実酒シーズン到来です。

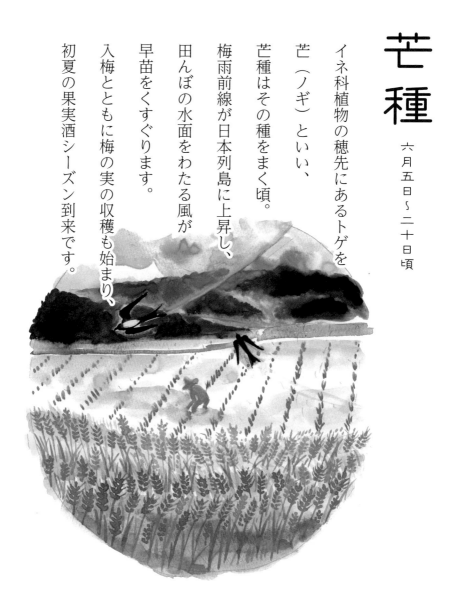

Boushu   Around June 5 to 20

The thorns at the tips of gramineous plants are called "Nogi (芒)", and Boushu tells the time to sow their seeds. The seasonal rainy front rises to the Japanese archipelago, with wind across the rice field surfaces rustling young sprouts.

The harvest of plum fruits begins when the rainy season comes, and the season for making early summer fruit wines has also arrived.

梅仕事と変わり梅酒

＊梅は古来貴重な保存食品で、さまざまに加工されてきました。各産地の出荷時に、まとめて作っておきたいもの。梅干しや梅酒のほか、梅ジュースや梅ジャムを作っておくと、暑い夏に重宝します。

＊スタンダードな梅酒のほかに、さまざまにアレンジできるのが梅酒のいいところ。おすすめは、ブランデー梅酒、紫蘇梅酒、ソルダム梅酒、松竹梅酒など。あなたもオリジナル梅酒を作ってみては。

Plum work and plum wine varieties

*Plums have long been a valuable preserved food and have been processed in various ways.You might want to make such preserved foods in a large quantity when plums are shipped from each production area.In addition to Umeboshi and Umeshu, making plum juice and plum jam would turn to be a right choice in hot summer.

*The best part of Umeshu is that it can be arranged in various ways in addition to the standard Umeshu.Recommended are brandy umeshu, shiso umeshu, soldum umeshu, or shochiku umeshu.Try making an original umeshu too.

【桑の実＆梅の実】

明治からの殖産興業を支えた養蚕と製糸は、お蚕様と桑の木のおかげ。子供たちのおやつ代わりになったドドメ（桑の実）も、今では懐かしい思い出。桑の実に梅の酸味を加えて果実酒に仕立てます。

Mulberry & Plum

Morus alba & Purunus mume

Silkworms and mulberry trees made possible the sericulture and silk-thered manufacturing that supported the promotion of industry from the Meiji period.Mulberries which were loved by children as a snack, are now a nostalgic memory. Plums add a sour taste to mulberries, making them into a fruit liquor.

桑の実梅酒　Mulberry & Plum Liquor

～濃赤紫がさえた郷愁の野生果実酒～
- A beautiful deep-reddish-purple wild fruit wine that brings back old memories -

＊桑の実‥‥‥‥‥‥‥300ｇ　＊梅の実‥‥‥‥‥‥ 200ｇ
　Mulberry　　　　　　　　　　　Plum

＊氷砂糖‥‥‥‥‥‥‥‥‥‥‥‥‥‥‥‥‥‥‥ 150ｇ
　Rock sugar

＊35度ホワイトリカー ‥‥‥‥‥‥‥‥‥‥‥‥ 900ml
　35% white liquor

＊桑の実は黒く熟したものを採取し、梅は果肉を厚くむいて種ごと入れます。
　Collect mulberries that became black and ripened. Peel the plums thickly and add them with their seeds inside of the pulp.

▼１～２ヶ月。1－2 months.
■ロック、水割り、炭酸割り。On the rocks, with water or soda.

★桑の実酒は、熟果と赤い未熟果を混ぜたり、レモンを加える方法も。
★Ripe and unriped red mulberries can be mixed, and lemons can also be added.

【枇杷】

枇杷は暖地を好む植物で、初冬に花を咲かせ5〜7月に熟します。枇杷の名は、葉や果実が楽器の琵琶に似ているからとか。果実のほか、葉は昔から薬用にされ、江戸時代には枇杷葉湯を売り歩く商売も。

Loquat *Eriobotrya japonica*

Loquats are a plant that prefer warm weather, and bloom in early winter and ripen during May-July.It is said that the Japanese name "Biwa " came from its appearance of leaves and fruits, which resembles the instrument "Biwa". In addition to fruits, leaves have been used for medicinal purposes from the old days. There was the business of peddling loquat leaf tea in the Edo period.

夏

壱種

ビワ酒　Biwa Liquor

〜家庭果樹のビックリ美酒〜
- A liquor made of a fruit from your backyard, which amazes you with its sophisticated taste -

＊ビワ……………………… 1 kg　＊氷砂糖……………… 200 g
Loquat　　　　　　　　　　　　Rock sugar
＊35度ホワイトリカー ……………………………… 1800ml
35% white liquor
＊ビワは皮をむかず、そのまま用います。
Not remove the skin of the loquats.

> ▼ 1 年熟成。Age the liquor for one year.
> ■ロック、炭酸割り。On the rocks or with soda.

★枇杷酒は酸味が少ないのでレモンや梅を 2 割ほど加えても。
★枇杷酒には市販品より庭先に忘れられた小粒のビワがよい。これは種から香り成分が出るからです。
★Loquat liquor has little sourness, so you can add lemons or plums for about 20%.
★For loquat liquor, small loquats that are left in the garden are better than commercial products.This is because the scent component comes from seeds.

夏至 六月二十一日〜七月六日頃

1年でもっとも太陽が高く
日が長いのが夏至。
日本ではまだ梅雨の真っ盛りで、
ドクダミが白い花を咲かせます。
半夏生もこの時季で、
烏柄杓（カラスビシャク‥半夏）が
生える頃。葉が半分白くなる
半化粧（ハンゲショウ）はドクダミの仲間。

Geshi [Summer Solstice]　Around June 21 to July 6

In the summer solstice, the Sun reaches its highest position in the sky and the day has the longest period of daylight in the year.

In Japan, the rainy season is still at its peak, and fish mint blooms white flowers.

Hangesyo also appears in this season, when crow-dippers grow.

Asian lizard's tail (or "Hangesyo"), of which half part of leaves turns white, is a varieties of fish mint.

ベリー類‥木苺とスグリ

＊ベリー類とは小型の果実をさす英語圏の言葉で、様々な種類を含みます。主なものにキイチゴ類、スグリ類、スノキ類、コケモモ類。

＊キイチゴは日本にも野生種がたくさんあり、黄色〜赤まで色も風味もさまざま。栽培品ではラズベリーとブラックベリーが有名。

＊スグリ類では、グーズベリーと房スグリの仲間のレッドカラントやブラックカラント（カシス）が知られます。

Berries: Brambles and Redcurrants

*Berries are English words that refer to small fruits and contain many varieties.The well-known berries include , raspberries, currants, vaccinium, and cowberries.

*There are a lot of wild species of raspberries in Japan, and the color varies from yellow to red and so does the flavor.Raspberries and blackberries are famous for their cultivation.

*For currants, redcurrants and blackcurrants (cassis), kinds of gooseberries and cultivated redcurrants are well-known.

【杏】

アンズは中国原産で、5000年前から栽培されていた果物。梅が終わる頃に熟し、昔は子供のおやつでしたが今は少なくなりました。ジャムのほか乾燥果実やシロップ漬けで、お菓子などに利用されます。

Apricot *Prunus armeniaca*

Apricots are a fruit native to China and have been cultivated over 5000 years.They ripen around the end of the plum blossom season and used to be a snack for children.In addition to jam, its dried fruits or syrup pickles are used for sweets, etc.

アンズ酒 Apricot Liquor

～香り立つ杏仁の匂いが魅力の美酒～
-An elegant liquor with fragrance of apricot -

＊アンズ Apricot	1 kg	＊氷砂糖 Rock sugar	150 g
＊35度ホワイトリカー 35% white liquor			1800ml

＊アンズは色の濃いものを選び、丸のまま用います。
Choose apricots with a deep color and use it as they are; no particular processing needed.

▼1年熟成。Age the liquor for 1 year.
■ロック、炭酸割り。On the rocks or with soda.

★杏林伝説：古代中国、貧乏な村人を無料で診察した名医の土地に、患者がお金の代わりにアンズの苗を植え、それが美しい杏の林となった。この故事にちなみ、杏林は名医の代名詞。★アンズの種子が杏仁で、呼吸器系の生薬にし、杏仁豆腐の香りづけにも使われます。★Legend of Kyorin (杏林): In ancient China, there was a good doctor who examined poor villagers free of charge. Patient planted apricot seedlings instead of money in the doctor's land, which became a beautiful forest of apricots.In connection with this legend, "Kyorin" is synonymous for a famous doctor.★Apricot kernels are the seeds of apricots, which are used as herbal medicines for the respiratory system, and are also used to scent almond jelly.

【ラズベリー】

キイチゴ属の代表がラズベリー。フランスではフランボワーズと呼ばれ、ソースや製菓に多用されます。キイチゴ類では断トツで香りがよく、女性好みの華やかな香りと鮮赤色は果実酒素材に最適。

Raspberry *Rubus idoeus*

Raspberries are the representative of the genus Rubus. In France, it is called "framboise" and is often used for sauces or sweets. Among the genus Rubus, its fragrance is second to none. Its gorgeous aroma and the fresh red color, which catch women's heart, are the best for the fruit liquor ingredients.

ラズベリー酒　Raspberry Liquor

～傑出した芳香のルビーレッドのプリンセス～
- A ruby-red princess outstanding with its gorgeous fragrance -

* ラズベリー…………200g　* 氷砂糖………………… 50g
  Raspberry　　　　　　　　　　Rock sugar
* 35度ホワイトリカー ………………………………… 600ml
  35% white liquor
* ラズベリーは崩れやすいので、浸すように洗い水を切っておく。
  Raspberries are easy to crumble, so soak them in water to wash then drain.

▼ 1週間以内。Within 1 week.
■ ロック、炭酸割り。On the rocks or with soda.

★色も香りも劣化しやすいので、早めに飲みきりましょう。
★Its color and fragrance are easily deteriorated, so drink it as soon as possible.

小暑

七月七日〜二十一日頃

小暑は、梅雨が明けて夏の暑さが始まる頃。

実際の梅雨明けは小暑の後半ですが、

七夕祭りを皮切りに

朝顔市や鬼灯市など

夏の行事も始まります。

蒸し暑さが増す季節には

爽やかな青色が恋しくなるもの。

Shousho　Around July 7 to 21

Shousho falls on about the end of Tsuyu in which summer heat begins.

Actually, Tsuyu ends in the second half of Shosho, around which summer events such as markets of Japanese morning-glories or Chinese lantern plants begin, following the Tanabata Festival.

In the season when the steaming heat increases, you will miss the fresh blue color.

44

【夏の薬味と香辛料】

＊暑い季節になると食欲を刺激するスパイスやハーブが重宝します。夏のハーブと言えば爽やかなミント類、トマトと相性がいいバジル。ミントティーやイタリアン料理に、鉢植えでも重宝します。

＊日本でも薬味として香味野菜を直接いただく知恵があります。青唐辛子や山椒・大葉・生姜・ニンニク・青ネギ・茗荷・辛味大根に生辣韭（ナマラッキョウ）。食の国際化で香菜（シャンツァイ・パクチー）やレモングラスも。

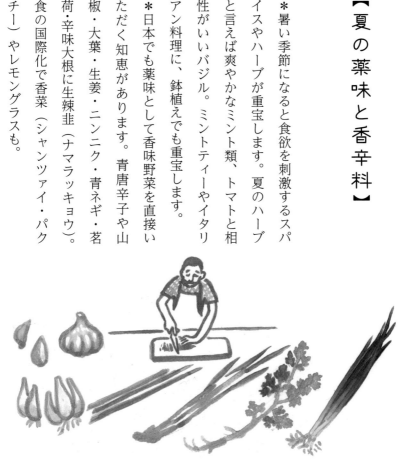

Summer condiments and spices

*Spices and herbs that stimulate appetite come in handy in the hot season.Speaking of summer herbs, fresh mint and basil go well with tomatoes.Potted basil and mint are useful for making mint tea and Italian dishes.

*In Japan, there is a wisdom of directly eating flavored vegetables as a condiment.Green pepper, sansho, oba, ginger, garlic, green onions, myoga, karami daikon and shallots. The internationalization of food has made coriander and lemongrass popular in Japan.

ブルーベリーはツツジ科スノキ属の小低木。青黒く熟す小果が可愛らしく女性に人気があり、あっという間に日本中に広まりました。日本には同じ仲間の野生種クロマメノキ（浅間ブドウ）が自生します。

Blueberry   *Vaccinium spp.*

Blueberries are small shrubs classified in the Vaccinium of the Ericaceae.The small fruit that ripens in blue and black is so pretty that it's popular among women, and it spread all over Japan in no time.In Japan, the wild species of the same kind, northern bilberries (Asama grape) grow naturally.

ブルーベリー酒　Blueberry Liquor

～青い小粒が赤紫の滴に結晶～
- Blue small berries crystalize into red-purple drops -

＊ブルーベリー‥‥‥‥‥‥‥‥‥‥‥‥‥‥‥ 300 g
　Blueberry

＊レモン果肉‥‥‥‥ 1/2個分　＊氷砂糖‥‥‥‥‥‥‥‥‥ 50 g
　lemon pulp　　　　A half　　　Rock sugar

＊35度ホワイトリカー ‥‥‥‥‥‥‥‥‥‥‥‥ 600ml
　35% white liquor

＊レモンは皮を厚めにむいて果肉をスライスし、果肉だけ使う。ブルーベリーはかるく浸す程度に洗い、水気をきる。
　Peel the lemon thickly, slice and use the pulp only.Wash the blueberries lightly in water and drain them.

▼ 1～2ヶ月。 1 to 2 months.
■ロック、炭酸割り、梅酒ブレンド。 On the rocks, or with soda, or in blend with plum wine.

★品種改良が進んでいますが、酸味の強い品種がおすすめです。
★早く仕上げたい場合、ブルーベリーを凍結して漬ける方法も。
★There are many improved varieties, but using one with strong acidity is recommended.
★If you want to finish the liquor quickly, you can also freeze the blueberries before steeping.

【ラベンダー】

富良野のラベンダー畑で一躍脚光を浴び、ハーブブームとともに日本各地で栽培されるように。シソ科ラベンダー属の総称で、香料やポプリに使われる一般的なものがイングリッシュラベンダー。

Lavender　*Lavandula officinalis*

As the lavender fields of Furano became popular, more and more lavender became cultivated in various parts of Japan along with the herb boom.English lavender is a general term for Lavandula, which is commonly used for fragrances and potpourri.

ラベンダーワイン　Lavender wine

～碧い芳香をまとったフラワーワイン～
- Flower wine with a bluish fragrance -

＊ラベンダー……………　15g　　＊氷砂糖………………　40g
　Lavender　　　　　　　　　　　　Rock sugar

＊ワイン(赤・白・ロゼお好みで) …………………………　300ml
　Wine (any of red, white, rose, you like)

＊35度ホワイトリカー　…………………………………　300ml
　35% white liquor

＊ハーブティー用のラベンダーはそのまま使えます。
　Lavender for herbal tea can be used without any processes.

▼1週間以内。Within 1 week.
■ロック、ストレート、炭酸割り。On the rocks, straight, or with soda.

★栽培品を採取する場合は無農薬を確認して。
★ミント類を少量加えても爽やか。
★If you use cultivated products, make sure that they are pesticide-free.
★Adding a small amount of mint makes the liquor refreshing.

大暑　七月二十二日～八月六日頃

いよいよ暑さのピークを迎え、
蝉時雨とともに子供たちは夏休み。
夏山、虫取り、
海水浴にスポーツ合宿。
大人だって暑気払いに
ビール＆枝豆、
花火見物に浴衣姿のお嬢さん。
打ち水に風鈴、梅酒で涼めばエコ＆風流。

Taisho　Around July 22 to August 6

The heat finally reaches at its peak, and children enter summer vacation with Semishigure (a big rain sound, unique to summer).

Climbing, insect hunting, swimming in the sea, sports camps, etc.

Adults enjoy beer, edamame, and fireworks. Some ladies wear yukata to cool down.

If you cool down with pouring water, wind chimes and plum wine, it's ecofriendly and tasteful.

夏土用とスタミナ食

＊土用は年に４回あり、立春・立夏・立秋・立冬の前の18日間ですが、普通は立秋前の夏土用を指します。土用といえば丑の日の鰻で、江戸の発明家・平賀源内の広告コピーとか。

＊『土用の食い養生』といって「う」のつく食べ物がよいといわれます。鰻、うどん、梅干し、瓜（きゅうり）、牛、馬。他にも土用蜆、土用餅（あんころ餅）、土用卵と、精のつく食べ物で暑さに対処。

Natsudoyo and Foods for Stamina

*Doyo comes four times a year, which falls on 18 days before Rissyun, Rikka, Rissyuu, Ritto, but usually refers to for Natsudoyo before fall.When it comes to Doyo, eels of the Ox day are famous of which custom is said to be an advertisement copy of the inventor in the Edo period, Gennai Hiraga.

*It is said that eating the foods with "u" in its name is good for health, which is called "Doyo-no-kuiyoujyou".Such as unagi (eel), udon, umeboshi, uri (cucumber), ushi (cow), uma (horse).Deal with the heat having the foods to increase your stamina like Doyo basket clams, doyo mochi (ankoro mochi), Doyo eggs.

【ソルダム】

ソルダムはスモモ（プラム）の仲間。果皮は緑で白い粉をふき、果肉が濃紅色で特徴的。大型で甘味・酸味・果肉の硬さもほどよく美味しい。梅の酸味がクエン酸なのに対し、スモモ類はリンゴ酸が主体です。

Soldum *Prunus salicina*

Soldum is a member of Asian plums.The peel is green with white powder on the surface, and the pulp color is characteristic dark red.The pulp is also large and very delicious with moderate sweetness, acidity, and hardness.While plums have citric acid, Asian plums have mainly malic acid.

ソルダム酒 Soldum Liquor

～野趣に富んだ赤い果実酒～
- A red fruit liquor rich in wild taste -

＊ソルダム…………………400ｇ ＊氷砂糖………………… 50ｇ
　Soldum　　　　　　　　　　　Rock sugar
＊35度ホワイトリカー ………………………………… 720ml
　35% white liquor
＊ソルダムは削ぐように大きくカットし、種ごと入れます。
　Cut the soldum in large size and put them in the bottle with the seeds being inside.

> ▼2ヶ月。 2 months.
> ■ロック、炭酸割り、水割り、梅酒ブレンド。On the rocks, or with soda, water, or in blend with plum wine.

★梅酒にソルダムを同量加えて漬けると、酸味もほどよく色も美しいブレンド果実酒に。
★When the same amount of soldum is added to the plum wine and steeped, the acidity is moderate, making a blend fruit wine of beautiful color.

＊梅……………………………………………………… 500ｇ
　Plum
＊ソルダム …………… 500ｇ ＊氷砂糖……………… 500ｇ
　Soldum　　　　　　　　　　Rock sugar
＊35度ホワイトリカー ……………………………… 1800ml。
　35% white liquor

【紫蘇】

紫蘇は、その葉を煎じて飲ませた病人が蘇ったことに由来するとか。赤シソ・裏赤シソ（赤シソの一種）と青シソがあり、さらに葉が平らな平シソと表面がシワの縮緬シソに。色の赤シソ、香りの青シソ。

Shiso *Perilla frutececens*

The name "Shiso" is said to be originated from the legend thata sick person who drank tea made of the roasted leaves revived.There are red shiso, back-red shiso (a kind of red shiso) and green shiso, and they are further divided into one with flat leaves and one with wrinkled-surface leaves.Red shiso for color and green shiso for fragrance.

シソ酒　Shiso Liquor

〜爽やかな和風ハーブ酒〜
- A refreshing Japanese-style herbal liquor -

＊シソ·················· 60 g
Shiso

＊レモン果肉·········· 1 個分
Lemon pulp　　　For 1 piece

＊35度ホワイトリカー ··· 720ml
35% white liquor

＊ （氷砂糖·········· 50 g 前後）
（Rock sugar　　　About 50g）

＊シソは水気をよく切り、レモンは皮をむき果肉をスライス。
Drain the shiso well, peel the lemon and slice the pulp.

▼2週間。 2 weeks.
■ロック、水割り、梅酒ブレンド。暑気払い、食前酒に。On the rocks, with water or in blend with plum wine.For cooling down or an aperitif.

★赤シソの場合、梅があればレモンの代わりに実をカットして加えると美味しい。また、赤・青ブレンドもおすすめ。
★When using red shiso and if you have plums, try putting their cut pulp instead of lemon, which makes the liquor more delicious.Blending red and blue shisos is also recommended.

立秋 八月七日～二十二日頃

暑いさなか、時折吹く涼風に
秋の気配を感じる時候。
とはいえ暑さも夏祭りも真っ盛り、
夏休みで帰省に旅行と。
月遅れ盆が過ぎる頃に
やっと空気が変わり、
濃い霧とともに
虫の音も聞こえ始めます。

Rissyuu　　Around August 7 to 22

It is the season when the approaching of autumn is felt in cool winds which blow occasionally in the hot weather.

On the other hand, the severe heat remains and a lot of summer festivals are held still, with people being busy with a travel or going back home in summer vacation.

The air finally changes when the a-month-late Obon passes, and the sound of insects begins to be heard in the thick fog.

夏の果菜と果実

＊夏の果菜類は水分とミネラルをいっぱい含んでいて、のどの渇きを癒やす作用も。ペットボトル飲料全盛の現代ですが、熱中症予防には生のキュウリやトマトに塩をつけてかじるのもおすすめです。

＊スイカは自然のスポーツドリンク、夏休みの子供たちのおやつにぜひ。後味もスッキリして、体の熱を冷ます作用もあり◎。

＊盆棚に飾られたメロンは子供の頃のあこがれ。送り火の後に食べた味は格別でした。昔に比べ手に入りやすい価格になりました。

Summer Vegetables and Fruits

*Summer vegetables and fruits contain a lot of water and minerals, and also have the effect of quenching thirst.It is an age of plastic bottle drinks, but try to bite raw cucumbers and tomatoes with salt. It is good to prevent heat stroke.

*Watermelons make a natural sports drink, and is recommended for a children's snack during summer vacation.The aftertaste is also refreshing, having an effect of cooling down the body.

*Melons on Obon shelves used to be a longing in childhood.The taste after Okuribi was exceptional. The pricing decreased to be more affordable compared with the old days.

【桃】

桃は中国原産で栽培歴史が古く、邪気を祓い不老長寿を得られる縁起の良い果物として有名。日本には弥生時代に渡来し、古事記や桃太郎伝説に登場するほど古い果物。とろける食感と芳香が好まれます。

Peach *Prunus persica*

Peaches are native to China and have a long history of cultivation, famous as a good luck fruit that expels evil and brings longevity.It came to Japan during the Yayoi period and is an old fruit that appears in Kojiki and the Legend of Momotaro.Melting texture and aroma are much loved.

モモ酒 Peach Liquor

～甘く芳醇なくつろぎの美酒～
- A sweet and fragrant relaxing liquor -

＊モモ······················500g
Peach

＊氷砂糖··················60g
Rock sugar

＊35度ホワイトリカー ································· 900ml
35% white liquor

＊モモは適当に削ぎ切りし、種が離れるものは、種を割って仁を使います。離れないものはそのまま入れます。
Cut the peaches appropriately. For ones of which seed can be detached, cut a seed and use its kernel.Put others with their seeds attached.

▼1ヶ月。 1 month.
■ロック、炭酸割り。 On the rocks, or with soda.

★食用にならない花桃の実も果実酒に利用できます。
★The fruit of flower peaches, which is inedible, can also be used for making fruit liquor.

Kumazasa　*Sasa veitchii*

Kumazasa has been used for food packaging for a long time because of its antiseptic effect and handiness."Kumazasa" does not refer to a single species, but a general term for large Sasa, which frames the edge of the leaves with white color in winter.They are also called "Kumazasa ('kuma' means a bear)" since bears after hibernation eat them for detoxifying.

【隈笹】

隈笹は防腐効果や素朴さで、昔から食品の包装に使われてきました。クマザサという単一の種はなく、大型で冬場に葉の縁を白く隈どる笹の総称。冬眠明けのクマが解毒に食べることから熊笹とも。

クマザサ酒　Kumazasa Liquor

～笹団子風味の意外なおいしさの野草酒～
- A surprisingly delicious wild grass liquor with sasadango flavor -

＊クマザサ………… 20枚ほど　＊30度甲類焼酎 …… 800ml
　Kumazasa　　　About 20 leaves　　30% korui shochu

＊（氷砂糖……………… 40ｇ）
　(Rock sugar)

＊30度甲類焼酎は、25度甲類焼酎と35度ホワイトリカーを半々で。
　The 30% korui shochu can be replaced with 25% korui shochu and 35% white liquor for each half amount.

＊クマザサは清浄区域のものを採取。絞ったタオルなどで葉の裏表を拭いて、3～4等分に切って用います。
　Choose Kumazasa trees which are planted in a clean area.Wipe the surface and backside of the leaves with a squeezed towel and cut them into equal 3-4 pieces.

▼1ヶ月。1 month.
■ロック、水割り。甘味を加えると蜜のよう。On the rocks, or with water. When sweetened, it tastes like honey.

★クマザサは7～9月のものがおすすめです。野草茶にも。
★笹草や真竹など、竹笹の仲間は果実酒にできます。
★It is recommended to collect Kumazasa in the period from July to September.Also for wild grass tea.
★Members of bamboo sasa such as Sasakusa or Madake can be made into fruit wine as well.

処暑　八月二十三日〜九月六日頃

夏の猛暑もやわらぎほっと一息、
朝晩は過ごしやすくなる時候。
梨や葡萄のくだもの狩りもそろそろ。
二百十日や八朔（旧暦八月一日）は
野分（ノワキ・台風の古称）が
来やすい日で、
注意が必要な時季とも。

Shosho　Around August 23 to September 6

The intense summer heat has been weakened, which allows people to take a breath for a while. Weather in morning and evening become moderate as well .

It's about time for picking pears or grapes.

Nihyakutoka (or "the 210th day") and Hassaku (August 1 of the lunar calendar) are days when typhoons often come and people should pay attention to them.

ツツジ科のベリー類

＊ブルーベリーやクランベリー（ツルコケモモ）に代表されるツツジ科スノキ属のベリー類は、冷涼な気候を好むものが多く、高山帯に多くみられます。晩夏の山登りついでに、少量を摘んで果実酒に。

＊日本では、コケモモ、ナツハゼ、クロマメノキ、ツルコケモモなどが有名。また、近い仲間のシラタマノキ属にアカモノ（イワハゼ）やシラタマノキが。

Ericaceae Berries

*Many of the berries of the Vaccinium of the Ericaceae, which is represented by blueberries and cranberries, prefer a cool climate and are often seen in alpine belts.
While climbing a mountain in late summer, pick a small amount of berries and make fruit wine.
*In Japan, Kokemomo, Natsuhaze, Kuromamenoki and Tsurukokemomo are well-known.
Also, the close members of the genus Gaultheria include Iwahaze and Shiratamanoki.

【木天蓼】（マタタビ）

木天蓼はキウイフルーツと同じ仲間の落葉つる性植物。山や沢沿い、林の縁に見かけ、若い葉は半分白いので遠くから目立ちます。先の尖った長楕円形が正常果で、虫癭果（チュウエイカ）は凸凹円盤状に変形。

Silervine　*Actinidia polygama*

Silvervines are a deciduous vine plant in which Kiwifruit is also included.They are found in mountains, along rivers, on the edge of forests, of which young leaves stand out from a distance because their half part is white.The figure of normal fruit is a pointed oval. If invaded by worms, the fruit is deformed into an uneven disk shape ("Tyueika").

マタタビ酒　Silvervine Liquor

～猫だけでなく人にも効く？野生の元気酒～
- Does it work not only for cats but also for people? A wild-taste energetic liquor-

＊マタタビ……………150ｇ
Silvervine
＊氷砂糖………………… 50ｇ
Rock sugar
＊35度ホワイトリカー …………………………………… 720ml
35% white liquor

＊正常果はつるから採取しますが、虫癭果は落果しやすいので拾い集めてよく洗います。
Normal fruit is taken from vines, but worm-invaded fruit is easy to fall off. So pick them up on the ground and wash well.

▼３ヶ月～１年熟成。Mature the liquor for 3 months to 1 year.
■ロック、水割り、梅酒ブレンド。On the rocks, with water, or in blend with plum wine.

★猫ちゃんのお土産には、果実のほか茎葉も効果があります。
★虫癭果は木天蓼（モクテンリョウ）という生薬で、鎮痛や強壮に利用。
★In addition to the fruit, leaves and stems are effective for cats.
★Tyueika is used as a herbal medicine called Mokutenryo, which is effective as analgesia and a tonic.

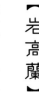

【岩高蘭】

寒冷帯に生え、日本では高山帯や北海道に自生するツツジ科の常緑小低木。ブラシ状に葉をつけ、密に分枝した群落はクッションのよう。5〜8㎜ほどの球果を密生してつけ、黒紫に熟します。

Gankouran *Empetrum nigrum*

It is an evergreen shrub of Ericaceae that grows in cold zones, native to the alpine belts and Hokkaido in Japan.With the brush-like leaves, a group of densely branched shrubs looks like a cushion.It bears ball-shape fruit of about 5 to 8 mm densely, which ripen in black purple.

ガンコウラン酒　Gankouran Liquor

〜魅惑のガーネットと幽玄な香気の傑品〜
- A masterpiece of enchanted garnet and mysterious aroma -

＊ガンコウラン⋯⋯⋯⋯200g
Gankouran
＊レモン果肉⋯⋯⋯ 1/2個分
Lemon pulp　　　　A half
＊氷砂糖⋯⋯⋯⋯⋯⋯⋯ 50g
Rock sugar
＊35度ホワイトリカー ⋯⋯⋯⋯⋯⋯⋯⋯⋯ 720ml
35% white liquor

＊丁寧に摘んだガンコウランは、水に泳がすように洗ってザルに取り、新聞紙などに広げて水気をとります。レモン果肉はスライス。
Wash the gankouran, which you carefully picked, in water gently and put in a strainer and drain on newspapers, for example.Slice the lemon pulp.

▼1〜3ヶ月。1 to 3months.
■ロック、炭酸割り、水割り。On the rocks, or with soda or water.

★高山帯の野鳥たちの貴重な食糧なので採り過ぎに注意。
★They are precious foods for wild birds in the alpine belt, so be careful not to take too much.

白露

九月七日〜二十一日頃

残暑も終わって
秋の空気に入れ替わり、
朝露を結ぶ時候。
赤とんぼが群れをなし、
藤袴や女郎花（オミナエシ）など
秋の七草も野山を彩ります。
9月第3月曜は敬老の日。
健康寿命と生き甲斐に果実酒つくりを。

Hakuro　Around September 7 to 21

It is the season when the afterglow has been over and the air is changed to that of autumn with dews formed in the morning. Red dragonflies flock and seven representative autumn plants, such as Fujibakama or Ominaeshi, color fields and mountains.
Respect for the Aged Day falls on the third Sunday of September. Make fruit wine as a hobby to lengthen healthy life expectancy and increase the pleasure of life.

長寿薬膳酒

高麗人参酒‥オタネニンジン（薬用人参・朝鮮人参）の薬膳酒。日本では最も有名な生薬で、効能は折り紙付き。

枸杞酒‥クコの実をほしたものが枸杞子。中国や韓国では不老長寿の妙薬とされ、昔から酒に醸して飲まれる薬膳酒です。

五味子酒‥チョウセンゴミシの実の薬膳酒。高原の半日蔭地に自生し、秋に小さな赤い実を葡萄の房状につけます。

五加皮酒‥ウコギの根皮を干したものが五加皮（ゴカヒ）。単味酒のほか、いくつかの生薬をブレンドした五加皮酒も市販されます。

Medicinal Liquor for Longevity

Ginseng Liquor: A medicinal liquor made of Otaneninjin (medical ginseng or Korean ginseng).It is the most famous herbal medicine in Japan with proven effectiveness.

Kuko Liquor: the fruit of Kuko is dried into "Kukoshi".In China and Korea, it is thought as a miracle medicine for longevity, brewed in alcohol and drunk since the old ages.

Gomishi Liquor: A medicinal liquor made of the fruit of Tyosengomishi.They grow naturally in the half shady place of plateau, bearing small red fruit like a bunch of grapes in autumn.

Gokahi Liquor: "Gokahi" is made from dried root skins of Ukogi.Gokahi liquors into which some herbal medicines are blended is also commercially available as well as one of single component.

漬け物などにする生姜を掘り取る季節。親生姜（根生姜）とはちがった瑞々しさと爽やかな風味が特徴で、この時期に是非漬けたい一品です。生姜の品種は気にせず、地元で採れるものを使いましょう。

Young ginger　*Zingiber officinale*

This is the season to dig up ginger, which is used for pickle making. It is characterized by a refreshing flavor and fresh taste that are different from those of Shinshoga. This ingredient is especially recommended for steeping in this season.Don't worry about the varieties of ginger. Use ones that can be available in your local area.

新生姜酒　Young ginger Liquor

〜香りと辛さが新鮮な薬膳酒〜
- A medicinal liquor featuring its aroma and spiciness -

＊新生姜 ……………………………………………… 200 g
　Young ginger
＊35度ホワイトリカー ……………………………… 720ml
　35% white liquor
＊新生姜は2〜3㎜にスライスします。
　Slice the young ginger into 2 to 3 mm pieces.

▼1〜2ヶ月。1 to 2 months.
■ロック、お湯割り、水割り。胃腸の不調や冷えに。On the rocks, with hot water or water. For curing your upset stomach and intestines, and cold.

★女性などで甘味が欲しい方は、氷砂糖や蜂蜜を原酒の10％前後の重さで加えましょう。
★If you want some sweetness as often women do, add rock sugar or honey for quantity of an around 10% weight of the base liquor.

【無花果】

無花果はクワ科の果樹でトルコ原産。メソポタミアでは六千年以上前から栽培されたとか。アダムとイブの腰蓑の葉で、生命力や知識、再生や豊かさの象徴とされ、不老長寿の果物ともいわれます。

Fig *Ficus carica*

Figs are a fruit tree of Moraceae, native to Turkey. It is said that it was cultivated in Mesopotamia more than 6,000 years ago. It is a leaf of grass skirt Adam and Eve wear, considered to be a symbol of vitality, knowledge, reproduction and abundance, which is also said to be a fruit of longevity.

イチジクワイン Fig Wine

～飲むイチジクコンポート～
- A fig compote for drinking -

＊イチジク……………300ｇ
Fig

＊氷砂糖………………… 40ｇ
Rock sugar

＊35度ホワイトリカー ………………………300ml
35% white liquor

＊レモン果肉……… 1/2個分
Lemon pulp   A half

＊赤ワイン………… 300ml
Red wine

＊イチジクは皮ごと縦４等分に切り、レモンは皮を厚めにむき果肉をスライス。
Cut figs into 4 equal pieces per skin, and peel the lemon skin thickly and slice the pulp.

▼2週間～１ヶ月。2 weeks to 1 month.
■ロック、炭酸割り。On the rocks, or with soda.

★濾したイチジクは、砂糖と水を足して煮るとコンポートに。
★Boiling filtered figs with sugar and water added makes them into compote.

秋分

九月二十二日～十月七日頃

春分と同じく、
昼と夜の長さが同じになる
秋分は秋のお彼岸。
田んぼが黄金色に変わり始め、
畦には真っ赤な彼岸花も。
空気が澄んでススキの
海に昇る中秋の名月は、
本格的な秋の訪れを感じさせます。

Shuubun [Autumn equinox]　Around September 22 to October 7

Same as the spring equinox, the autumn equinox, where the length of day and night are the same, is the day of autumn Higan.
Rice fields begin to turn golden with bright red Higan flowers seen on the ridges.
The mid-autumn moon, which rises in the sea of Susuki in clear air, makes you feel the real coming of autumn.

薬用人参の仲間

薬用人参…御種人参（オタネニンジン）とも呼ばれ、江戸時代に徳川吉宗が栽培を奨励した輸入生薬。虚弱衰弱の万能生薬として有名です。

三七人参（サンシチニンジン）…田七（デンシチ）とも呼ばれ、中国南部が原産地。特に血を巡らせる作用が強く、肝臓疾患に有効とか。

栃葉人参（トチバニンジン）…生薬名は竹節人参（チクセツニンジン）で、日本原産。山地の木陰などに自生し、根茎が竹の節のように伸びます。

西洋人参…アメリカ人参とも。北アメリカ原産で、原住民に利用されていたものをイエズス会宣教師が発見。薬用人参の陽性に対し、陰性の性質をもつといわれます。

Member of medicinal ginseng Panax

Medicinal Ginseng is also known as "Otane Ginseng", which was imported as herbal medicines that General Tokugawa Yoshimune encouraged to grow in the Edo period.
It is a well-known cure-all medicine for improving a weak physical constitution or curing collapse.

Sanshichi Ginseng: Also known as "Denshichi", native to southern China. It is said that it has a special strong effect of increasing blood circulation and effective against liver disease.

Tochiba Ginseng: Its herbal medicine is called "Chikusetsu Ginseng", which is native to Japan. It grows naturally in the shade of trees in the mountains, and their roots grow like bamboo joints.

Western Ginseng: Also called "American Ginseng". It was discovered by a missionary of the Society of Jesus, which is native to North America and was once used by natives. It is said to have a negative property while medical ginseng has a positive property.

【猿梨】

マタタビやキウイフルーツの仲間で、本州では山間部に自生する雌雄異株の蔓木。北海道ではコクワと呼ばれ、緑の俵型果実が熟すと芳香を放ちヒグマの大好物です。最近はベビーキウイの名で栽培も。

Sarunashi *Actinidia arguta*

It is a kind of silvervines and kiwifruit, which is a dioecious vine and grow naturally in the mountainous areas in Honshu.In Hokkaido, it is called "Kokuwa", of which green mulch-shaped fruit giving off fragrance when it ripens is a favorite of brown bears.Recently, it is also cultivated with a name "baby kiwi".

サルナシ酒 Sarunashi Liquor

～深山の芳香ただよう琥珀の滴～
- A drop of amber with aroma of deep mountain -

＊サルナシ‥‥‥‥‥‥300ｇ　＊氷砂糖‥‥‥‥‥‥‥‥40ｇ
　Sarunashi　　　　　　　　　　　Rock sugar
＊35度ホワイトリカー ‥‥‥‥‥‥‥‥‥‥‥‥‥‥‥ 720ml
　35% white liquor
＊サルナシは収穫後数日おき、芳香が出て少し軟らかくなってから漬けます。
　Leave the sarunashi for few days after harvest before steeping to allow its aroma to come out and make the fruit a little softer.

▼半年～1年。6 months to 1 year.
■ロック、水割り、炭酸割り。On the rocks, or with water or soda.

【金木犀】

9月下旬から10月上旬にかけて
オレンジ色の小花を咲かせ、
芳香を辺り一帯に漂わせる金木犀。
中国原産の雌雄異株で、日本は雄株だけ。
中国では丹桂と呼ばれ、
白ワインに漬け込んだ桂花陳酒は有名。

Kinmokusei　*Osmanthus fragrans*

From the end of September to the beginning of
October, Kinmokusei blooms orange-colored
flowers of which fragrance wafts throughout
the area.It is dioecious and native to China, and
only males exist in Japan.In China, it is called
"Tankei" and famous for its white wine-soaked
"Keikachinshu".

秋

秋分

キンモクセイ酒　Kinmokusei Liquor

〜甘味を抑えた手作り桂花陳酒〜
- Handmade Keikachinshu with less sweetness -

＊金木犀の花‥‥‥‥‥‥‥‥‥‥ 900mlビンにほぼいっぱい
Kinmokusei flowers　　　　　　　　Full of 900ml bottle

＊氷砂糖‥‥‥‥‥‥‥ 40ｇ　＊白ワイン‥‥‥‥‥ 300ml
Rock sugar　　　　　　　　　　White wine

＊35度ホワイトリカー ‥‥‥‥‥‥‥‥‥‥‥‥‥‥ 300ml
35% white liquor

＊咲き始めた金木犀の花を早朝に摘み、さっと水にくぐらせて
しっかり水を切ります。
Pick Kinmokusei flowers that has begun to bloom early in the morning, and
then quickly dip them into water and drain the water thoroughly.

> ▼１週間〜１ヶ月。1 week to 1 month.
> ■ロック、炭酸割り。金木犀香が素晴らしい。On the rocks, or
> with soda.The osmanthus fragrance is wonderful.

★花の白い銀木犀や晩秋に咲く柊（ヒイラギ）の花も香りがよく、
花酒に。
★White flowers of Ginmokusei, and flowers of Hiiragi, which
bloom in late autumn are also fragrant, suitable to make
flower wine.

寒露 十月八日～二十二日頃

虫の音が寂しさを増し、
露も冷たさを増してくる寒露。

「秋は夕暮れ」

釣瓶落としの夕陽に映える
夕焼けが美しい頃。

澄んだ空気に冴える月や
薫る菊を愛でるのも一興。

稲刈りや山の茸も盛りを迎えます。

Kanro   Around October 8 to 22

Kanro is the season when the sound of insects is heard in withering fields and haze becomes colder.

"In autumn, sunset is especially beautiful," the sky that passes over as quickly as a bucket falling in a well shines beautifully in the sunset.

It's also tasteful to see fragrant chrysanthemums and the moon that shines in the clear air.

People are busy at harvesting rice and mountain mushrooms.

菊の節句と登高（とうこう）

＊旧暦9月9日は菊の節句（重陽節句）。中国では、高い所に登って菊花酒を飲む習慣があったようです。後漢時代、費長房という仙人が弟子の恒景の災難を予言し、茱萸（グミ）を入れた赤い布袋を腕に巻いて9月9日には家を離れ、高所に登って菊花酒を飲むように伝え、恒景一家が難を免れたことに由来します。なお、ここでの茱萸は山茱萸（サンシュユ）か呉茱萸（ゴシュユ）と思われます。

Kiku-no-Sekku and Toukou

*Kiku-no-Sekku falls on the 9th of September of the lunar calendar (or called "Chouyou"-no-Sekku), in which people used to climb high places and drink chrysanthemum liquor in China. It is originated from the episode in the later Han period that the hermit named Hi Chobo predicted the calamity of his disciple Kokei and then he told Kokei to leave his house on September 9th with a red cloth bag of Gumi (silverberries) wound on his arm and climb up to a high place and drink chrysanthemum liquor, which helped Kokei's family escape the difficulty. The gumi in this story is thought to be Sanshuyu or Goshuyu.

【柘榴】

柘榴は遠くトルコから中央アジア周辺が原産。世界で広く栽培され、果肉からジュースやグレナデンシロップを作ります。古代ギリシャ・ローマ時代は多産の象徴とされ、子供のいない女性が食べたとか。

Pomegranate *Punica granatum*

Pomegranates are native to around central Asia and Turkey at their furthest point.Widely cultivated around the world, their pulp is made into juice or grenadine syrup.In the ancient Greek and Roman periods, they were considered as a symbol of prolific birth, and were eaten by women without children.

ザクロ酒 Pomegranate Liquor

～シルクロードの魅惑の美容酒～
- An enchanted beauty liquor from the Silk Road -

＊ザクロの果肉‥‥‥‥‥300ｇ
Pomegranate pulp

＊氷砂糖‥‥‥‥‥‥‥‥‥40ｇ
Rock sugar

＊35度ホワイトリカー ‥‥‥‥‥‥‥‥‥‥‥‥‥‥ 600ml
35% white liquor

＊ザクロの実を割って、粒々の果肉を取り出します。
Break the pomegranate fruit and take the grain pulp.

▼１ヶ月。 1 month.
■ロック、炭酸割り、水割り。 On the rocks, or with soda or water.

★ザクロには女性ホルモン様作用のある成分が微量含まれているようですが、美容効果などは他の成分が寄与している模様。
★It is said that pomegranates contain a small amount of components that have an effect resembling those of female hormones, but other components are considered to contribute to its beauty effect.

【菊花】

秋といえば菊というように日本的な花として愛されていますが、元々は中国原産です。菊は古来観賞用に広く栽培され、品評会や菊人形展など催しも多い花。観るだけでなく味覚でも楽しみましょう。

Chrysanthemum

Chrysanthemum morifolium

The expression "autumn is all about chrysanthemums," means that Chrysanthemums are loved as a Japanese flower of autumn, but it is originally native to China.Chrysanthemums have been widely cultivated for ornamental purposes since ancient times, and there are many events such as competitive exhibitions and chrysanthemum doll exhibitions.Enjoy not only seeing but also tasting them.

菊花酒　Chrysanthemum Liquor

～緊張を和らげ余熱を除く薬膳酒～

- A medicinal liquor to relieve tension and exclude excess heat -

＊食用菊 ················· 50ｇ 　＊(氷砂糖 ············· 50ｇ)
Edible chrysanthemums　　　　　　　(Rock sugar)

＊35度ホワイトリカー ······································· 600ml
35% white liquor

＊菊花は水に浸してかるく水洗いし、水気をきります。
Soak the chrysanthemums in water and wash lightly and drain.

▼1週間。1 week.
■ロック、水割り、お湯割り。お月見に一杯。On the rocks, with water or hot water.Take a sip at moon viewing.

★中国の菊花酒は数種の生薬を一緒に漬け、1年寝かせて作ります。
★菊花酒には香りの強い白か黄色の中～小菊がおすすめですが、農薬を使っていなければ色・形は問いません。
★Chrysanthemum liquor in China is made by soaking several kinds of herbal medicines together and maturing for a year.
★It is recommended to use white or yellow medium-small chrysanthemums with a strong fragrance for making chrysanthemum liquor, but if pesticides are not used, color and size do not matter.

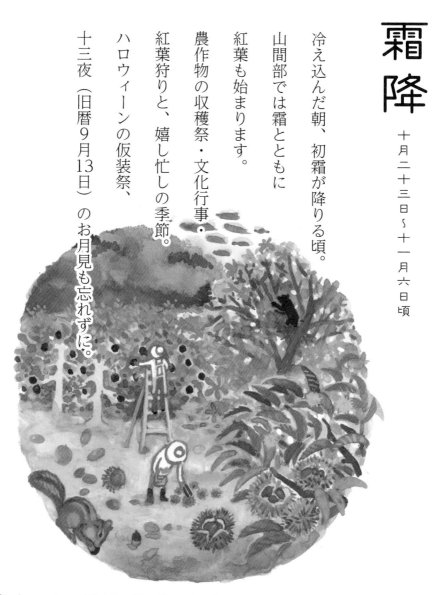

霜降 十月二十三日〜十一月六日頃

冷え込んだ朝、初霜が降りる頃。

山間部では霜とともに紅葉も始まります。

農作物の収穫祭・文化行事。

紅葉狩りと、嬉し忙しの季節。

ハロウィーンの仮装祭、

十三夜（旧暦9月13日）のお月見も忘れずに。

Soukou   Around October 23 to November 6

In this season, the first frost is seen in the very cold morning.
In the mountains, leaves begin to turn red with the frost.
People are happy and busy having harvest festivals, cultural events, maple-tree viewing.
Don't forget to see the moon on the 13th night (September 13th in the lunar calendar),
or join the Halloween costume festival.

ハロウィーン

＊元々は古代ケルト人の秋の終わりの収穫祭だったハロウィーン。20世紀に入ってアメリカで普及し、日本には1990年代に入ってきました。当初は注目されませんでしたが、2010年代に入ると仮装パーティーとしてブレーク、秋の一大イベントに定着しました。

Halloween

*Halloween was originally an ancient Celtic harvest festival held at the end of autumn. It became popular in the United States in the 20th century and came into Japan in the 1990s.Initially, it was not noticed, but in the 2010s it became popular as a costume party, and was established as a major event in autumn.

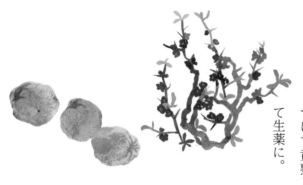

【木瓜】

ボケは早春を彩る花木で中国原産。古くから庭木や盆栽で栽培され、赤花が一般的ですが園芸品種も多数あります。木瓜は木に生える瓜の意味で、秋に硬い実をつけて黄熟し、木瓜（モッカ）と呼ばれて生薬に。

Boke *Chaenomeles speciosa*

Boke is a flower tree that is native to China and decorates early spring.It has been cultivated in garden and as bonsai since ancient times. Red flowers are common, but there are also many horticultural varieties.The name "Boke" means a gourd that grows on tree. In autumn, the fruit is hard and ripened yellow, called "Mokka", which came to be used as herbal medicine.

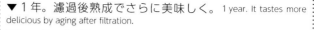

ボケ酒 Boke Liquor

～冷え・不眠・疲労によい薬膳佳酒～
- A medicinal liquor good for coldness, insomnia, and fatigue -

＊ボケの実‥‥‥‥‥‥‥‥200g ＊氷砂糖‥‥‥‥‥‥‥‥‥ 80g
　Boke fruit　　　　　　　　　　　Rock sugar
＊35度ホワイトリカー ‥‥‥‥‥‥‥‥‥‥‥‥‥‥‥‥ 600ml
　35% white liquor
＊果実を半分に切り、5㎜ほどにスライスします。
　Cut the fruit in half and slice it into about 5 mm each.

▼1年。濾過後熟成でさらに美味しく。 1 year. It tastes more delicious by aging after filtration.
■ロック、水割り。On the rocks, or with water.

★黄色く熟した果実がよく、落果も使えます。青いものは追熟させてから。虫が入ったものは、そこだけ取り除けば利用可。
★野山に自生するクサボケの実もシドミや地梨（ヂナシ）と呼ばれ、美味しい果実酒になります。
★Yellow ripe fruit is desirable. Fallen fruit can be used as well.Leave the blue ones to ripen.Even worm-eaten fruit can be used if you remove the parts.
★Fruit of Kusaboke native to wild mountains is also called "Shidomi" or "Jinashi", which can be good fruit wine ingredients.

Kougyoku　*Malus domestica*

It is an apple variety that came in from the United States in the early Meiji era. It used to be a major variety, but its production volume much decreased now due to popularity of the other new varieties. Kougyoku, an apple with red-black peel and a strong sour taste are ideal for making sweets or baked apples.

【紅玉】

明治初期にアメリカから入ってきたリンゴ。かつての主要品種で一世を風靡しましたが、新品種に押されて今は生産量が激減。赤黒い果皮で酸味の強い紅玉は、加工用として製菓や焼きりんごに最適です。

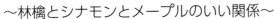

焼りんご風紅玉酒　Kougyoku Liquor with Baked Apple Taste

〜林檎とシナモンとメープルのいい関係〜
- A good relationship between apple, cinnamon and maple -

＊紅玉·················350 g Kougyoku	＊シナモンスティック··· 1本 Cinnamon　　　　　　　　1 stick

＊氷砂糖·················· 30 g
Rock sugar

＊メープルシロップ·································· 大さじ2
Maple syrup

＊35度ホワイトリカー ································· 720ml
35% white liquor

＊リンゴは皮ごと四つ割りにし、さらに5㎜ほどにスライスします。シナモンスティックは粗く砕きます。
Cut the apples into four pieces with their skin attached and slice them to about 5mm each.

▼1〜2ヶ月。1 to 2 months.
■ロック、炭酸割り。香ばしいデザート酒。On the rocks, or with soda. A fragrant dessert wine.

★生姜のスライスを加えると、健胃や温め効果が増します。
★リンゴを食べるときに捨ててしまう皮と芯だけを漬ける方法や、種だけ集めて漬ける香りのお酒も。
★Adding a slice of ginger will increase effects of enhancing the stomach activity and warming the body.
★You can also steep the skins and cores only that are typically thrown away, or the seeds only to make a flavored liquor.

秋
霜降

立冬 十一月七日〜二十一日頃

朝晩冷えて暖房が恋しくなり、
囲炉裏や炬燵を開いて
冬の準備を始める頃。
紅葉も山から里に下り
木々を染め上げます。
華やかに着飾った子供たちは
七五三のお宮参り。
鷲（オオトリ）神社の酉の市も賑わいます。

Rittou   Around November 7 to 21

It gets cold in the morning and evening, and people set iori or kotatsu to prepare for winter.
Autumn leaves descend from mountains to villages, dying trees.
The children dressed gorgeously visit the shrine to celebrate Shichigosan.
The fairs at the Otori Shrine are also crowded.

紅葉する葉

＊紅葉といえばカエデの仲間。

広葉モミジ、羽団扇楓（ハウチワカエデ）、瓜肌楓（ウリハダカエデ）、目薬の木。

ウルシ科のハゼノキ、山漆（ヤマウルシ）、蔦漆（ツタウルシ）、ヌルデ。

他にも錦木や山桜、ナナカマド、更紗満天星（サラサドウダン）、ブルーベリー。

里に目をやれば、イロハモミジ、染井吉野、柿、欅、低木では満天星躑躅（ドウダンツツジ）や南天も。

＊黄葉するものでは、

一葉楓（ヒトツバカエデ）、花の木、栃ノ木、ユリノキ、山鳴らし、そして公孫樹（イチョウ）。

冬

立冬

Trees that turn red

*Maples are most common as trees that turn red.Examples include broad-leafed maple, Hauchiwakaede, Urihadakaede, Nikko maple.Members of Anacardiaceae, Hazenoki, Yamaurushi, Tsutaurushi, Nurude.Others include Nishikigi, Yamazakura, Nanakamado, Sarasadoudan, Blueberries.In villages, you will find Irohamomiji, Somei Yoshino, persimmons, Keyaki, and for shrubs, Doudan Azaleas and Nanten.
*The yellow-leafed ones include Hitotsubakaede, Hananoki, Tochinoki, Yurinoki, Yamanarashi, and ginkgos.

【国産レモン】

瀬戸内海沿岸や島々を中心に栽培されている国産レモンが出回る頃。皮ごと使える新鮮な国産レモンなら、レモン本来の良さを生かした調理が可能です。マーマレードや砂糖漬け、塩レモンも今でしょう。

Lemon from Japan　*Citrus limon*

It is the time when lemons in Japan grown mainly on the coast or islands of the Seto Inland Sea appear in the market.Lemons produced in Japan can be cooked with its skin attached, so you can cook making use of the original taste of lemons.It is the best season for making marmalade, candied and salted lemons.

国産レモン酒　Home Grown Lemon Liquor

〜青春のほろ苦さと酸っぱさが甦る〜
- A liquor bringing back the bitter, sour memory of adolescence -

＊レモン……………………200ｇ　　＊氷砂糖………………… 30ｇ
　Lemon　　　　　　　　　　　　　　　Rock sugar
＊35度ホワイトリカー ……………………………………… 600ml
　35% white liquor
＊レモンは皮を削ぐようにむき、白いワタを取り除いて果肉をスライスします。皮と果肉を使い、ワタは入れません。
　Peel the lemons, remove the white stuffs and slice the pulp.Use the peels and pulp, but not the white stuffs.

▼１〜２ヶ月。1 to 2months.
■ロック、水割り、炭酸割り。On the rocks, with water or soda.

★輸入レモンは数種類の防カビ剤が使われていて、皮は使えません。
★苦味が苦手な方は、皮だけ１週間ほどで引き上げましょう。
★Don't use peels of imported lemons since several types of antifungal agents are used.
★If you mind bitterness, take the peels in about a week.

【洋梨】

ねっとりした食感と芳香、独特の形が特徴の洋梨は、リンゴとともに晩秋が旬。収穫してからしばらく追熟させ、果肉が軟らかくなり香りが出てくると食べごろ。生食のほかコンポートや洋菓子にも。

Pear　*Pyrus communis*

Pears, which have a characteristic sticky texture, aroma and shape, become in season in late autumn along with apples. After harvesting, they are left to ripen for a while and become ready to eat when the pulp becomes soft and the aroma comes out. Not only for eating raw, but also they are used to make compote or sweets.

洋梨酒　Pear Liquor

～ほんのり洋梨香が上品なマイルド酒～
- A mild liquor with an elegant pear aroma -

* 洋梨·························300g
  Pear
* 氷砂糖·················· 30g
  Rock sugar
* レモン果肉········· 1/2個分
  Lemon pulp　　　　A half
* 35度ホワイトリカー ······················· 500ml
  35% white liquor: 500ml
* 洋梨は縦に4等分し、5mmくらいにスライス。レモンは皮を厚めにむき、果肉だけスライスして使います。
  Cut the pears vertically into 4 pieces and slice them to about 5mm each. Peel the lemon thickly, and slice and use the pulp only.

▼1～2ヶ月。1 to 2 months.
■ロック、炭酸割り、水割り。デザート酒に。On the rocks, or with soda or water. For dessert liquor.

★香りのよいラ・フランスがおススメ。
★It is recommended to use fragrant la france pears.

冬

立冬

小雪 十一月二十二日〜十二月六日頃

木枯らしが枯れ葉を舞い上げ、
小雪がちらついて高い山は
雪化粧を始める頃。
落ち葉の散歩も
心地良い季節。
勤労感謝の日は元の新嘗祭、
農家は収穫を祝って
神棚や屋敷神様に赤飯や新米をお供えします。

Shousetsu　Around November 22 to December 6

It is the time when the winter wind blows up dead leaves, and light snow falls on the ground, turning the top of high mountains white.It is also a pleasant season to take a walk in fallen leaves.On Labor Thanksgiving Day, originally the Niinamesai Festival, farmers offer red and new rice on a household Shinto altar to gods to celebrate harvest.

赤い実

*紅葉が散ると野山も冬木立に変わり、色を失った木々に赤い実を見つけると心がほっと和みますね。赤い実の中で果実酒や薬膳酒になるものを拾ってみました。山では七竈（ナナカマド）や酸実（ズミ・ガマズミ）、里では枸杞（クコ）や山茱萸（サンシュユ）。南天は咳止め、野茨は下剤に用いられますが、果実酒にはおすすめしません。

Red Fruit

*When autumn leaves fall, wild mountains are covered with withering trees. During such time, red fruit seen in the trees that have lost their color, your heart will be relieved.We picked up some red fruits that can be made into fruit wines and medicinal liquors.In mountains, you can find fruits of Nanakamado, Zumi, and Gamazumi, and in villages, Kuko and Sanshuyu.Nanten is used for cough medicines and Noibara as laxatives, but they are not recommended to use for fruit wine.

【キウイフルーツ】

キウイフルーツは、中国原産のシナサルナシ（彌猴桃ビコウトウ）がニュージーランドで品種改良されたもの。スタミナフルーツでビタミンCが豊富、タンパク質分解酵素を含むのでお肉との相性も抜群です。

Kiwifruit　*Actinidia deliciosa*

Kiwifruits are a variety of Chinese native Shinasarunashi which was improved in New Zealand.It is a fruit for stamina, rich in vitamin C and containing proteolytic enzymes, which make it well compatible with meat.

キウイフルーツ酒　Kiwifruit Liquor

～お肉料理の食前酒に～
- For an aperitif with meat dishes -

＊キウイフルーツ………300 g
Kiwifruit

＊レモン果肉…………　1 個分
Lemon pulp　　　For 1 piece

＊氷砂糖………………… 50 g
Rock sugar

＊35度ホワイトリカー ………………………… 600ml
35% white liquor

＊キウイフルーツは皮ごと薄く輪切りにします。レモンは皮を厚めにむき、果肉だけをスライスして用います。
Cut the kiwifruit into thin slices with its skin attached.Peel the lemon thickly, slice the pulp only to use.

▼１〜２ヶ月。 1 to 2months.
■ロック、水割り、炭酸割り。 On the rocks, or with water or soda.

★冷えやすい人は、生姜を加えるといいでしょう。
★If you are sensitive to cold, add some ginger.

【花梨】

のど飴で馴染みのある花梨は、中国原産で平安時代には日本に渡来。中国では模樝（メイサ）といい、漢方生薬名は和木瓜（ワモッカ）。果実は楕円形で黄色く熟し芳香を放ちますが、木質で硬く生食は無理。

Karin *Pseudocydonia sinensis*

Karin, which is often used in throat refreshing candies, is native to China and came to Japan during the Heian period.In China, it is called Meisa, of which name as herbal medicine is "Wamokka".The fruit is oval, ripens yellow and gives off fragrance, but is woody and hard, so you cannot eat raw one.

カリン酒　Karin Liquor

〜疲労回復によい琥珀の滴〜
- A drop in amber good for curing fatigue -

* カリン·················300 g
  Karin

* 氷砂糖·················80 g
  Rock sugar

* 35度ホワイトリカー ································ 600ml
  35% white liquor

* レモン果肉··········· 1個分
  Lemon pulp　　　　For 1 piece

* カリンはお湯で皮表面の汚れや皮脂をよく洗い落とし、縦半分に切ってから5㎜くらいにスライスします。種も捨てないこと。レモンは皮を厚めにむき、果肉だけをスライスして用います。
  Wash off the dirt and oil on the skin surface well with hot water, cut them vertically in half, and slice to about 5mm.Don't throw away the seeds.Peel the lemons thickly and slice the pulp only to use.

▼3ヶ月〜1年。 3months to 1year.
■ロック、お湯割り、水割り。 On the rocks, or with hot water or water.

★カリンに似ているマルメロも美味しい果実酒になります。
★Marmelo, which is similar to Karin, is also made into a delicious fruit wine.

大雪 十二月七日〜二十日頃

山を白く染め、日本海側には
本格的な雪がやって来て、
鍋物が恋しくなる季節。
1年の総決算に
各地で年末市が開かれ、
忘年会や年末行事と
あわただしい年の瀬。
農家は沢庵や白菜・野沢菜の漬け込みも。

Taisetsu　Around December 7 to 20

It is the season when mountains are dyed white and heavy snow falls on the area along the Japan Sea, making people miss one-pot dishes.

Year-end markets are held in various places for the conclusion of the year, and people have a very tight schedule with year-end parties or events.

Farmers pickle dried radish to make Takuan, and Chinese cabbage or Nozawana.

【香酸柑橘類】

＊柑橘類のうち香りや酸味が強く、皮や果汁を料理の調味料や薬味として用いるものを香酸柑橘といいます。柚子のほか、秋刀魚の塩焼きや松茸に絞る酢橘（スダチ）やカボス、正月飾りに使う橙（代々）はポン酢に。沖縄産のシークワシャー、レモンやライム、シトロンなどの仲間です。果実酒にもなりますが、苦味に注意しましょう。

Flavorful acid citrus fruits

*Among citrus fruits, it is called flavorful acid citrus fruits that the aroma and acidity are strong, and the skin and juice are used for seasonings or condiments in cooking.In addition to Yuzu, Sudachi and Kabosu, which are used for seasoning salt-grilled autumn sauries or matsutake mushrooms, or Daidai, which is used for Syogatsu decorations, can be made into ponzu. Other members include Hirami-lemons, lemons, limes, citrons, etc.Fruit wines can be made from them, but be careful with their bitterness.

【柚子】

日本の柑橘類では最も寒さに強い柚。柚は木を指し、果実は柚子または柚酸が正式とか。日本人好みの爽やかな芳香で、日本料理、柚餅子、柚子胡椒、お菓子の香り付けのほか、入浴剤や芳香剤にも。

Yuzu *Citrus junos*

Among Japanese citrus fruits, it is strongest in the cold.It is said that "Yu " refers to the trees and "Yuzu" or "Yunosu" is used to refer to the fruit.It has a refreshing aroma which Japanese people prefer and is used for scenting Japanese cuisine, yuzumochi, yuzu pepper, sweets as well as for bath salts and fragrances.

ユズ酒 Yuzu Liquor

～香り立つお湯割りの晩酌～
- A fragrant hot evening liquor -

＊ユズ ·· 4個
　Yuzu   4 pieces
＊25度甲類焼酎 ··· 1800ml
　25% korui shochu
＊ユズは白いワタをあまりつけないよう皮を薄めにむく。実は半分に切って汁を絞り茶こしで濾します。皮と果汁を利用。
　Peel the yuzu thinly so as not to allow too much white stuffs to attach.Cut the pulp in half and filter the juice with tea strainer.Use the peels and fruit juice.

▼1週間。1 week.
■お湯割り、水割り、ロック。With hot water and water, or on the rocks.

★小型の花柚、大型の獅子柚子（鬼柚子）も漬けられますが、風味は若干異なります。
★Small-sized Hanayu or large-sized Shishiyuzu (Oniyuzu) can be steeped, but the flavor is slightly different.

【メグスリノキ】

メグスリノキは日本固有のカエデ属で、秋には毛の生えた大きめの三枚葉が真っ赤に紅葉します。その名の通り、樹皮や小枝が目薬に利用され、財を成した歴史から、「千里眼の薬」や「長者木チョウジャノキ」とも。

Megusurinoki　*Acer nikoense*

Megusurinoki is a genus of maples unique to Japan, and in autumn, its large, hairy three-piece leaves turn red. As the name suggests, bark and twigs are used for eye drops, and from the history of people making a fortune with them, it is also called a "medicine of second sight" or "Nikko maple".

メグスリノキ酒　Megusurinoki Liquor

～スッとしたクセのない飲み口～

＊メグスリノキ樹皮・小枝‥‥‥‥‥‥‥‥‥‥‥‥ 20 g
　Megusurinoki bark and twig
＊リンゴ‥‥‥‥‥‥‥‥ 250 g ＊氷砂糖‥‥‥‥‥‥‥‥ 30 g
　Apple　　　　　　　　　　　　Rock sugar
＊35度ホワイトリカー ‥‥‥‥‥‥‥‥‥‥‥‥‥ 600ml
　35% white liquor
＊メグスリノキは粗く砕き、リンゴは４つ割り後５㎜くらいにスライスします。
　Coarsely crush the bark and twigs, cut the apples into four pieces, and slice them to about 5mm pieces.

▼１～２ヶ月。1 to 2 months.
■ロック、炭酸割り、水割り。On the rocks, or with soda or water.

★晩酌用には、メグスリノキだけで25度甲類焼酎を使います。
★煎じてお茶にもされます。
★For evening drink, put only the megusurinoki ingredients into 25% korui shochu.
★It is also made into tea by roasting.

冬至

1年で夜が最も長く、
年の最後の時候が冬至。
かぼちゃを食べて柚子湯に入り
無病息災を祈ります。
クリスマス行事に
正月飾りを売る歳の市、
大掃除、お節料理も完成し、
大晦日は年越し蕎麦で除夜の鐘。

Touji[Winter Solstice]　Around December 21 to January 4

Touji is the last season of the year in which night is longest in a year.
People have pumpkins and take a bath of yuzu, praying for a disease-free life.
Tons of events and parties are coming up in the end of the year, not mention to Christmas, markets selling New Year's decorations, end-year cleaning, and Osechi preparation are all finished, and enjoy Toshikoshisoba listening to Joya-no-kane.

冬至の風習

*冬至といえば柚子湯と冬至南瓜カボチャ（唐茄子トウナス）ですが、ほかにもいくつもの風習が残っています。

*冬至粥（小豆粥）は厄払い、蒟蒻（コンニャク）は体の砂出し（体内の掃除）。冷酒（ヒヤザケ）、豆腐、唐辛子、泥鰌（ドジョウ）、けんちん汁やいとこ煮。

*「ん＝運」が付く食べ物の盛り合わせを供える「運盛り」という行事もあったよう。特に「ん」が重なる銀杏（ぎんなん）・人参（にんじん）・蓮根（れんこん）・南瓜（なんきん）・金柑（きんかん）・寒天（かんてん）・饂飩（うんどん）が冬至の七種ナナクサ。

Customs of Touji

*Speaking of Touji, a bath of yuzu, Touji pumpkin (tou eggplant) are famous, but there are still many other customs.

*People have Touji porridge (Azuki porridge) to prevent misfortune and have konnyaku to clean the body.Other foods include Hiyazake, tofu, chili pepper, weather loaches, Kenchin soup and Itokoni.

*It is said that there used to be an event called "Unmori (accumulating fortune)" in which the assortment of foods with "ん (n)" in their names is offered ("運" meaning "fortune" is pronounced "u-n" in Japanese).In particular, Ginnann, Ninjin, Renkon, Nankin, Kinkan, Kanten, Undon, in which "n" appears twice are the indispensable seven ingredients for Touji.

【ローズマリー】

ローズマリーは「海の滴」という意味のラテン語。葉に独特の樹脂香があり、ジビエ(狩猟肉)や肉料理の臭い消しには最適のハーブです。「若返りのハーブ」とも呼ばれ、婦人科系やストレス、老化予防にも。

Rosemary　*Rosmarinus officinalis*

The name "Rosemary" came from Latin, meaning "a drop in the sea". The leaves have a unique resin aroma and is the best herb to remove smell of wild game meat and other meats.Also known as "rejuvenation herbs", it is used for curing gynecological disease, reliving stress, and preventing aging.

ローズマリーワイン　Rosemary Wine

～女性にやさしいハーブワイン～
- A women-friendly herbal wine -

＊ローズマリー小枝······················· 10㎝×3〜5本
　Rosemary twig
＊氷砂糖·················· 50g　＊赤ワイン·············· 360ml
　Rock sugar　　　　　　　　Red wine
＊35度ホワイトリカー ································· 360ml
　35% white liquor
＊茂っているローズマリーの枝の先端を10㎝ほど切り取り、水洗いして水気をふき取ります。
　Cut the tips of rosemary twigs for about 10cm and wash them with water and drain.

▼3日〜1週間。3days to 1week.
■ストレート、ロック、炭酸割り。Straight, on the rocks, or with soda.

★オレンジピールやミカンの皮、シナモンスティックやクローブを加えるとサングリア風に。
★Add orange peels, tangerine skins, cinnamon sticks or cloves to make a sangria taste.

【金柑】

金柑は皮ごと生食できる小型の柑橘で、甘露煮や蜂蜜漬けが有名。咳止めのほか疲労回復・風邪予防・健胃作用もあり、風邪の季節に重宝します。ここでは、柚子の香りとレモンの酸味を足した薬膳酒で。

Kinkan *Fortunella margarita*

Kinkan is a small citrus that can be eaten raw with skin, and is famous for its kanroni and honey-pickle.It is highly valued in the season of colds and has effects of stopping cough as well as curing fatigue, preventing a cold, and enhancing the stomach activity.Here, we introduce a medicinal liquor to which flavor of yuzu and acidity of lemons are added.

金柑柚子酒 Kinkan Yuzu Liquor

〜コク・酸味・香りの柑橘黄金ブレンド〜
- A golden blend of richness, sourness, flavor of citruses -

＊金柑‥‥‥‥‥‥‥‥‥200 g
Kinkan
＊柚子‥‥‥‥‥ 1 個分の皮
Yuzu　　　　　Peels of 1 piece
＊レモン果肉‥‥‥‥‥ 1 個分
Lemon pulp　　　 For 1 piece
＊氷砂糖‥‥‥‥‥‥‥‥ 60 g
Rock sugar
＊35度ホワイトリカー ‥‥‥‥‥‥‥‥‥‥‥‥ 720ml
35% white liquor
＊金柑は1/3 〜 1/4の輪切り、柚子は皮をむき、レモンは皮を厚めにむいて果肉を輪切りにします。
Cut the kinkan into 3 to 4 slices, peel the yuzu, and peel the lemon thickly and slice the pulp.

▼１〜２ヶ月。 1 to 2months.
■ロック、炭酸割り、水割り。 On the rocks, or with soda or water.

★柑橘類同士は相性がいいので、さまざまなブレンドを試してみましょう。ミカンの皮も候補に。
★Citruses are compatible with each other, so try different blends.Tangerine peels also make a good blend.

冬

冬至

正月

一月一日～三日

新しい年を祝うお正月。
いそがしい時代ですが、
お屠蘇を飲んで
御節やご馳走を食べて、
三が日くらいはのんびりしたいもの。
古来のお屠蘇は薬臭くてという方には、
手作り果実酒がおすすめです。

New Year   January 1 to 3

Shogatsu is New Year's Day to celebrate a new year.
We live in a busy world, but it is forgivable to spend a relaxing time, drinking Otoso, or
having Osechi in the first three days of the new year.
For those who mind a medicinal smell of traditional Otoso, a handmade fruit wine is
recommended.

お屠蘇

お屠蘇の発祥は中国三国時代に遡り、屠蘇散（屠蘇延命散）という生薬処方を酒や味醂に漬け込んだもので、名医・華佗が創ったとされています。華佗の文献は残っていませんが、『備急千金要方』（孫思邈581年）や『本草綱目』（李時珍1578年）に登場します。

日本でも平安時代には行われていたよう。

現代日本の調合は、山椒・桂皮・防風・桔梗・白朮の5種に生姜（ショウキョウ）・丁子（チョウジ）・陳皮（チンピ）など数種を加えたものが一般的。

冬
正月

Otoso

The origin of Otoso dates back to the Three Kingdoms period of China. Otoso was made by steeping a herbal medicine prescription called "Tososan (Tosoenmeisan)" in sake or mirin, which is said to be created by a famous doctor, Hua Tuo.There is no literature left about Hua Tuo, but he appears in "Qian-jin-fang" (Sun Si-miao, 581) and "Pen-tsao Kangmu" (Li Shih-chen, 1578).It is said that it was used in Japan in the Heian period.In modern Japan, it is common to mix five ingredients, Sansyo, Keihi, Bofu, Kikyou, and Byakujutsu, with several other seasonings such as Shoukyo, Choji, or Chimpi.

【山査子】

山査子はバラ科サンザシ属数種の果実で、肉や魚の消化不良の生薬として知られます。中国ではお菓子や飲料にも加工される秋の味覚。おなかの調子を整えるリンゴと合わせ、美味しくやさしい果実酒に。

Sanzashi *Crataegus spp.*

Sanzashi is a fruit of several species from Crataegus Rosacea, known as a herbal medicine helping indigestion of meat and fish.In China, it is a representative autumn food processed into sweets and beverages.Blending with apples, which have an effect of balancing the stomach condition, makes a delicious and healthy fruit wine.

サンザシりんご酒 Sanzashi Apple Wine

～食べ過ぎのお助け果実酒～
- A fruit liquor helpful to improve your condition in case of overeating -

＊山査子……………… 30 g
Sanzashi
＊リンゴ…………… 300 g
Apple
＊氷砂糖……………… 40 g
Rock sugar
＊35度ホワイトリカー ……………………………… 600ml
35% white liquor
＊リンゴは四つ割りにして5㎜くらいにスライス。山査子は漢方薬局などでカットしたものを購入してそのまま使います。
Cut the apples into four pieces and slice them into about 5mm pieces. Sanzashi in a cut form is available at a Chinese medicine pharmacy. No additional processing needed.

▼2週間～1ヶ月。 2 weeks to 1 month.
■ロック、お湯割り、水割り。On the rocks, with hot water or cold water.

★山査子は消化促進のほか血流改善にもよいようです。
★In addition to promoting digestion, Sanzashi enhances blood circulation.

門松や正月飾りに使われる目出度い植物の代表が松竹梅。中国の画題の一つ『歳寒三友』が由来で、冬に緑を保つ松と竹、初春に花を開く梅です。果実酒には赤松葉、竹の代わりに隈笹を使いました。

Shou-Chiku-Bai

Shou-Chiku-Bai represents the most auspicious plants used for Kadomatsu and New Year's decorations.It is derived from one of the Chinese paintings' titles, "Three Friends of Winter (or Saikan no Sanyuu)", which features a pine and bamboo, which keep green in winter, and a plum, which blooms in early spring.Leaves of Akamatsu and Kumazasa instead of bamboo are used for fruit wine.

松笹梅酒　Matsu-Sasa-Umeshu

～滋味豊かで縁起の良い薬膳梅酒～
- An auspicious medicinal plum wine with a rich taste -

＊梅‥‥‥‥‥‥‥‥‥‥1 kg　＊隈笹の葉‥‥‥‥‥10枚程度
Plum　　　　　　　　　　　　 Kumazasa　　　About 10 leaves

＊松葉‥‥‥‥鉛筆くらいの量　＊氷砂糖‥‥‥‥‥‥‥‥ 400 g
Pine needle　About a quantity of a pencil　Rock sugar

＊35度ホワイトリカー ‥‥‥‥‥‥‥‥‥‥‥‥‥‥‥ 1800ml
35% white liquor

＊6月に梅と氷砂糖とホワイトリカーで梅酒を漬け、7～8月に新葉が開いた隈笹と松葉を適当に切って加えます。
In June, make plum wine by steeping the plums and rock sugar in white liquor, and cut the leaves of Kumazasa and pine into appropriate sized-pieces, which opened in July and August to add into the plum wine.

▼正月前には飲む分だけ。残りは1年熟成。Make plum wine for a quantity to be consumed on New Year's Day.Age the rest for one year.
■ロック、水割り。On the rocks, or with water.

★松葉が多いとヤニ臭さが強くなるので控え目に。
★隈笹以外の竹笹類でも大丈夫。
★消化や血行促進のほか、老化や生活習慣病予防にも。
★If too many pine needles are put, the smell of pine resin might be very strong, so be careful.
★Other bamboo sasa may be used other than Kumazasa's.
★Effects of preventing aging and lifestyle related diseases are expected as well as those of promoting digestion and blood circulation.

小寒 一月五日〜一月十九日頃

小寒は寒の入りで、
一番寒い季節の始まり。
昔は七日の七草、
十一日の鏡開き、
あるいは十五日の小正月までは
松の内といい、正月気分でした。
各地に伝統行事も残っていて、
「初」が付く行事も目白押し。

Shoukan　Around January 5 to 19

Shoukan is the beginning of midwinter, the coldest season of the year.
Traditionally, a period from New Year's Day to January 7th for Nanakusa Gayu, or 11th
for Kagami Biraki, or 15th of the end of the Koshogatsu, is called Matsunouchi, in
which the Japanese celebrate a series of new year's events.
A lot of traditional events are observed in rural areas even these days, many of which
bear the word "first" at the top of the name.

【七草粥と黒五類】

＊1月7日は人日（ジンジツ）の節句、七草粥を食べて健康を願う習慣があります。七草が揃わなくても、青味の野菜で補えば十分です。

＊芹（セリ）、薺（ナズナ）、御形（ゴギョウ・母子草）、繁縷（ハコベ）、仏の座（ホトケノザ・小鬼田平子コオニタビラコ）、菘（スズナ・蕪）、蘿蔔（スズシロ・大根）

＊漢方では、冬は「腎経」が衰えやすく、黒い食品で補うのが良いとされ、黒五類：黒豆・黒胡麻・黒米・黒松の実・黒カリン（黒スグリの仲間）が珍重されます。

Nanakusa Gayu and Five Black Foods

*The Japanese have a custom to eat Nanakusa Gayu (rice porridge made with seven herbs) in January 7th wishing for good health.Even if you don't have all the seven herbs, you can go with other greenish vegetables.Seri, Nazuna, Gogyo, Hakobe, Hotokenoza, Suzuna, Suzushiro

*In Kampo, it is said that "the Kidney Meridian" tends to be weak in winter and should be nourished with black-colored foods like the highly-valued Five Black Foods: black beans, black sesame, black rice, black pine nuts, black Chinese quince.

小寒

【黒胡麻】

胡麻は熱帯アフリカが原産といわれ、古代エジプトやインドでも栽培されたとか。品種や系統は三千種にのぼり、色も白〜黄〜黄褐〜黒までさまざま。手軽な健康素材ですが、漢方では黒胡麻が珍重されます。

Black Sesame *Sesamum indicum*

Sesame is considered to be originated from Sub-Saharan Africa and cultivated in ancient Egypt and India.The types of varieties or systems amount to over 3,000 of which colors vary from white, yellow, yellow brown to black.While black sesame seeds are everyday healthy food, they are highly valued in Kampo medicine.

黒胡麻酒 Black sesame Liquor

〜香ばしさが癖になる不老長寿酒〜
- An elixir of life with roasting aroma you will surely be addicted to -

＊黒胡麻‥‥‥‥‥‥‥200ｇ ＊25度甲類焼酎 … 1800ml
　Black sesame seed　　　　　　25% korui shochu

＊黒胡麻はフライパンで煙が出るまでよく煎り、粗熱をとります。
Roast the black sesame seeds in a frying pan until it smokes and cool them down.

▼２週間〜６ヶ月。2 weeks - 6 months
■お湯割り、牛乳割り。晩酌向き。With hot water or milk.Suitable for evening drink.

★胡麻は粒の状態ではほとんど消化されません。よく噛むか、すり胡麻やペーストで。
★Sesame seeds themselves are hardly digested.Chew well, grind or make a paste.

黒豆は煮豆で御節に入る縁起物。大豆の品種のうち皮が黒いもので、黒大豆として薬用にも。珈琲はエチオピア原産で、今は世界中で愛されている飲料。含まれるカフェインやクロロゲン酸には興奮作用が。

Black Bean and Coffee
Glycine max & Coffea arabica

Black beans are a good luck charm that are boiled and put in Osechi.It is one of the soybean varieties which has a black skin and is also used for medical purposes.Coffee is native to Ethiopia and is now a beverage loved all over the world. Caffeine and chlorogenic acid contained have an excitatory effect.

黒豆コーヒー酒　Black-bean Coffee Liquor

～和洋折衷のカルーア～
- A Kahlua of Japanese and Western eclectic culture -

＊黒豆	150 g	＊コーヒー豆	30 g
Black beans		Coffee beans	
＊氷砂糖	80 g	＊25度甲類焼酎	720ml
Rock sugar		25% korui shochu	

＊黒豆はフライパンで皮が裂けるまでしっかり煎る。焙煎済みのコーヒー豆は粗挽きに。
Roast the black beans in a frying pan thoroughly until their skins are torn.For roasted coffee beans, grind coarsely.

▼半月から１ヶ月。Half month to 1 month
■牛乳割り。With milk.

★大豆にはサポニン、イソフラボン等、女性にやさしい成分も。黒豆の色はアントシアニン系色素。
★Soybeans contain nutrition especially good for women such as saponins and isoflavones.The color of black beans comes from anthocyanin pigment.

冬

小寒

大寒　一月二十日～二月三日頃

大寒は大地が凍てつく極寒の時候。

体を活性化して温める食品を

たくさん摂りたいもの。

葱やニンニク・生姜・

シナモンなどの薬味や香辛料、

柑橘類で元気に過ごします。

最終日は節分で、春遠からじ。

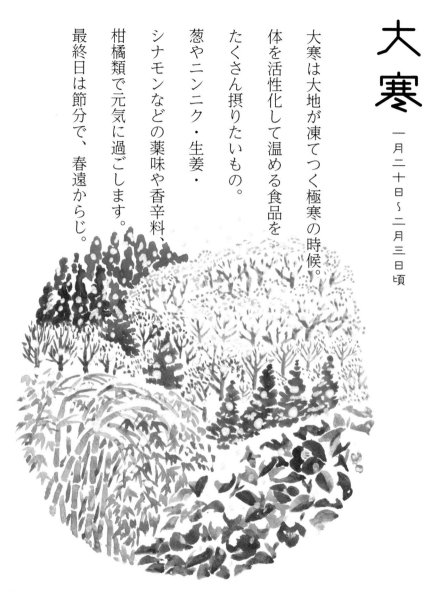

Daikan　Around January 20 to February 3

Daikan is a cold season when the earth freezes.
You might want to take a lot of food that activates and warms the body.
Condiments, spices, and citrus fruits such as welsh onion, garlic, ginger, and cinnamon
allow you to keep in good condition.
The last day of Daikan is "Setsubun", and spring is now not so far.

【節分と鬼と豆まき】

＊節分は、立春・立夏・立秋・立冬の前日にあたりますが、冬の終わりの節分が一般的。文字通り季節を分ける日で、古い季節の邪気を祓い新しい季節を迎える準備の日。

＊鬼門とされる北東(丑寅ウシトラ)は邪気が入る方向で、邪気の象徴の鬼は牛の角に虎のパンツ姿。玄関に飾る鰯の頭と柊は、鰯の頭の臭いと刺のある柊の葉で鬼の侵入を防ぐおまじない。

冬

大寒

Setsubun, Demons, and Bean-throwing

*Setsubun falls on the day before Rissyun, Rikka, Rissyuu, and Ritto, but the Setsubun at the end of winter is common.It is a day that literally divides seasons, and people ward off evil of the old season to prepare to welcome a new season .

*The north-east (or "Ushitora"), which is said to be a demon gate, is the direction where evil is entered, and demons, a symbol of evil, have cow horns and wear a tiger pants.The sardine head and Hiiragi which decorate entrances are a magic charm which prevents invasion of the demon by the smell of sardine head and stings of hiiragi leaf.

桂皮はシナモン属の一種、ニッキ飴や京都八つ橋の風味で知られる肉桂の仲間。熱帯アジア原産の生姜は、日本では薑（ハジカミ）と呼ばれた最も古い野菜の一つで、平安貴族は風邪薬にしていたとか。

Cinnamon & Ginger

Cinnamomum zeylanicum & Zingiber officinale

Cinnamon is a kind of Cinnamomum, and a member of Cinnamomum Cassia is known for flavor of Nikki candy and Kyoto Yatsuhashi. Ginger, native to tropical Asia, is one of the oldest vegetables called "hajikami" in Japan, and the Heian aristocrats used it as a cold medicine.

シナモン生姜酒　Cinnamon Ginger Liquor

～風邪と寒さにほかほか薬膳酒～
- A medicinal liquor for cold -

＊生姜·····················150ｇ　＊シナモンスティック… 2本
Ginger　　　　　　　　　　　Cinnamon　　　　　　　2 sticks
＊35度ホワイトリカー ······································· 720ml
35% white liquor
＊生姜は薄くスライスし、シナモンスティックは粗く砕きます。
Slice the ginger thinly and crush the cinnamon sticks coarsely.

▼半月～2ヶ月。Half month to 2 months.
■お湯割り、ロック、水割り。デザートにも。With hot water,
on the rocks, or with water.Also suitable for dessert.

★漢方で、シナモン類は温裏去寒（体の中を温めて寒さを除く作用）、
生姜は辛温解表（辛味で体を温め発汗させる作用）。
★In Kampo, cinnamon has an effect to warm inside of the body and remove cold, and ginger an effect to warm the body with pungency and proceed sweating).

【伊予柑】

ミカンと入れ替わりに登場する伊予柑は、甘く爽やかな芳香が特長で、栽培が広まった愛媛県の旧名に因んで命名。柑橘類は皮が命、捨てるのはモッタイナイ。料理や果実酒、芳香剤に利用します。

Iyokan　*Citrus iyo*

Iyokan, which comes in season following tangerines', has a characteristic sweet, refreshing aroma and is named after the old name of Ehime Prefecture where cultivation spread.The vital part of Citrus is its skin, so it is Mottainai to throw away.It is used for cooking, fruit wine, and fragrances.

伊予柑酒　Iyokan Liquor

〜甘い香りの柑橘焼酎〜
- Sweet-scented citrus shochu -

＊伊予柑 ･･････････ 1個分の皮　＊25度甲類焼酎 ･････ 800ml
　Iyokan　　　　　　1whole peel　25% korui shochu

＊伊予柑を丸ごと洗い、皮をそぐようにむきます。
　Wash the whole bodys of the Iyokans and shave the skins off.

▼5日。長く漬けると苦味が。5 days. If steeped for a too long time, it might be bitter.

■お湯割り、ロック。With hot water, or on the rocks.

★果肉を加える場合は房から取り出し、35度ホワイトリカーで氷砂糖を少量加えます。女性向きの甘い果実酒に。

★If you want to add the pulp, take it and add a small amount of rock sugar with 35% white liquor. They make a sweet fruit wine loved by women.

【果実酒作りの約束事】

●漬け込みビン●

＊アルコールを使ってさまざまな素材の成分を抽出するので、密封できるガラスビンをおすすめします。

＊ビンは洗って乾燥させておくこと。ジャムとかと違い、熱湯殺菌する必要はありません。

●漬け込み原酒●

＊素材の風味を生かす見地と価格から、ここではおもに35度や25度甲類焼酎（ホワイトリカー）を素材に合わせて選んでいます。

＊お好みで、ブランデーやウイスキー・ラム・ウオッカなどの蒸留酒でもかまいません。

＊ワインや紹興酒を使う場合は、アルコール度数が足りないので、35度ホワイトリカーと半々にブレンドしましょう。

[How to Make Fruit Wine]

●Steeping Container●

*You will extract components of various ingredients using alcohol, so it is recommended to use a grass bottle that can be sealed.

*Wash and dry the bottle beforehand.

Unlike jams, you don't need to sterilize with hot water.

●Unprocessed Original Wine●

*Considering the cost and the way to fully derive the original taste of ingredients, we suggest using 25% or 35% korui shochu (or white liquor) for each ingredient in this calendar.

*If you prefer, distilled liquors such as brandy, whiskey, rum or vodka may be used.

*If you use wine or Shaoxing wine, since their alcohol percentages are low, blend them with 35% white liquor for the half amount.

*In order to prevent fermentation of ingredients, using unprocessed original wine alcohol of 20% or less is prohibited by law.

＊素材が発酵するのを防止するため、20度以下の漬け込み原酒は法律で禁止されています。

●漬け込み素材●

＊基本的に毒草以外は漬けられますが、次のものは法律で禁止されています。

☆ブドウ・ヤマブドウ　☆穀物・芋類

＊輸入柑橘類において、防カビ剤を使っているものは、皮を使用できません。

＊大気汚染のひどいところや、土壌汚染の疑われるところに生育している素材は用いない。

●甘味料・酸味料●

＊ここでは原則、氷砂糖を使っていますが、白砂糖やグラニュー糖でもかまいません。

＊お好みで、黒砂糖・蜂蜜・メープルシロップなどを用いると、風味の異なる果実酒に仕上がります。

＊酸味の少ない素材では酸味を補うこともあります。酸味

●Steeped Ingredients●

*Basically, any ingredients except for poisonous grasses can be steeped, but the following are prohibited by law.

☆Grapes, Yamagrapes ☆grain, potatoes

*The skin of imported citrus fruits in which antifungal agents are used cannot be used.

*Don't use the ingredients that grow in areas where air pollution is severe or soil contamination is suspected.

●Sweeteners and acidulants●

*Basically, we introduce use of rock sugar here, but you can use white sugar or granulated sugar instead.

*If you like, use brown sugar, honey, maple syrup, etc. to make fruit liquors with different flavors.

*Acidity may be added for the ingredients with little acidity.

As acidulants, lemons are a handy choice, but the skin should be peeled thickly to use the pulp only.

It's because due to antifungal agents applied on imported lemons, but even for

料としてはレモンがお手軽ですが、皮を厚めにむいて果肉だけを使うようにしましょう。防カビ剤の問題と、国産品でもレモンの風味・苦味が出すぎるからです。

＊風味の関係もありますが、梅酒の時季なら梅をカットして用いる方法もあります。バラ科の果実や桑の実には合います。

▼漬け込み期間▼

＊標準的な期間を記しました。温度や砂糖の量・アルコール度数で変わってきますから、様子を見て濾すようにしましょう。

＊果実酒の失敗で一番多いのが濾し忘れです。漬けっぱなしで何年も置くと、素材の酸化変敗で色や香りが落ちます。漬けたら必ず濾して、飲んでください。果実酒は飾り物ではありません。

●漬け方●

＊素材の水洗いと水気をきることは共通なので、各素材の

---

domestic lemons, its flavor and bitter taste might be too strong.

*Flavor will be changed, but cut plums may be put instead if it is the season of plum wine.

It goes well with Rosacea fruits or mulberries.

▼Steeping Period▼

*The standard period is described below.

The period varies depending on temperature, amount of sugar and alcohol content, so filter the steeping liquor if it seems appropriate for the status.

*The most common failure in making fruit wine is to forget to filter the wine.

If you leave ingredients steeped for many years, the color and aroma will be deteriorated due to oxidation of the ingredients.

Once you steeped ingredients, make sure to filter the liquor and drink in an appropriate period. Fruit wine is not a decoration.

●How to Steep●

*It is a common process to wash and drain ingredients, so the process is omitted from

漬け方の項目から省略して、注意する場合だけ記しています。

＊保存は冷暗所が基本ですが、直射日光が当たらない常温なら特に問題ありません。冷蔵庫のような低温に置くと、抽出が遅れます。

＊濾すときは、ロート（すいかん）にペーパータオルやろ紙をつけ、用意した細口の４合ビンなどの口にさして濾します。

■ 飲み方 ■

＊風味を楽しむならストレートやオンザロックです。

＊水割り・お湯割り・ソーダ割りもおすすめです。

＊牛乳で割ると美味しいものもあります。（コーヒーやココアのお酒）

＊果実酒同士のブレンドもありです。酸味の少ないものと強いもの、風味の少ないものと香りのお酒。同じ仲間の素材のもの同士など。

the description of the steeping procedure for each ingredient. It is provided only when special attention is needed.
*Basically, liquors should be placed in a cool and dark place, but they may be left in any place if it is at room temperature and they are not exposed to direct sunlight.
Putting them in a place at a low temperature as that of refrigerator may slow down the extraction process.
*When filtering, put a paper towel or filter paper on a funnel, and put the funnel into a 4-go bottle with a narrow opening to filter the liquor.
■ How to Drink ■
*If you want to enjoy flavor, drinking straight or on the rocks is recommended.
*Drinking with water, hot water or soda is also recommended.
*Some of them are delicious with milk. (Coffee and cocoa liquor)
*You can blend fruit liquors. Try blending one with less sourness and one strong sourness, or one with less flavor and one with fragrance, or those made of ingredients of the same family.

＊果実酒は、濾して保存しても風味が劣化しやすいものが多いので、長期熟成すると色も香りも落ちてきます。なるべく早めに飲むことをおすすめします。一般的には、硬い果実の酒は長持ちし、軟らかい果実の酒は劣化が早い傾向です。

● 果実酒の楽しみ方 ●

＊旅先などで入手した珍しい素材を漬けると、飲むときに思い出がよみがえります。

＊結婚や子供の誕生・家族の記念日に合わせて果実酒を漬けて濾し、保存します。節目の年に開けて飲むと楽しいものです。この場合は、長期保存がきく梅酒などがおすすめです。

＊濾した果実酒を綺麗な小瓶に入れ、プレゼントに使うのもお洒落。ラッピングに凝れば、オリジナルのギフトにもなります。

*The flavor of many fruit liquors tends to be easily deteriorated even if they were filtered for storage, so quality of color and aroma will be lowered if aged for a long time.
It is recommended to drink as soon as possible.
In general, liquors made of hard fruits are long lasting, and ones made of soft fruits tend to be deteriorated quickly.

●How to Enjoy Fruit Wine●

*If you steep the rare ingredients you brought back with from a trip destination, you will remember the memory of the trip each time you drink.
*Steep, filter, and store fruit liquors so that you can serve them at occasions such as wedding, childbirth, or the anniversary of your family.
It is fun to open the bottle and drink to mark a year.
In this case, plum wine is recommended as they can be preserved for a long time.
*It is also stylish to put a filtered fruit liquor in a beautiful small bottle as a present.
Special wrapping will make it a unique gift.

★注意事項★

＊漬けた果実酒の販売は法律で禁止されています。

＊果実酒は甘いものが多く美味しいので、未成年者の飲酒に注意しましょう。特にお子様には与えないでください。

＊酒税法では、果実酒とはワインやシードルなど、果実を発酵させたものを指します。ここでいう果実酒は、リキュールなどの混成酒や浸漬酒という分類にあたります。

＊最後に、失敗しないため重ねて申し上げます。漬けたら→濾して→飲む　を必ず忘れずに、楽しく美味しい果実酒生活を満喫しましょう。「10年物の果実酒が漬けたまま眠っているよ」なんて自慢になりませんから、残念！

★Notes★

*Selling fruit liquors is prohibited by law.
*Many of Fruit liquors are sweet and very delicious, so be careful to prevent minors drinking.
In particular, do not give them to children.
*Under the Alcohol Tax Law, "fruit wine" refers to wine or cider made of fermented fruits.
"Fruit wine" here is classified as mixed or steeped liquor.
*Finally, we give an advice to ensure your success:
Don't forget the processes: steep ingredients, then filter the liquor, and drink it; to enjoy a life with delicious fruit liquors.
You can never boast "I have a fruit wine left and steeped for 10 years!

【おわりに】

私が生まれた当時、農家などで慣習的に作られていた梅酒は、厳密にいえば酒税法違反行為でした。

この悲しい現実に終止符を打つべく立ち上がったのが石田穣氏でした。内閣広報参与をしていた氏が、昭和36年『日本経済新聞』に梅酒礼讃論を堂々と寄稿し、大蔵省と国税庁を相手に論破して窮地に追い込みます。さらに世論の後押しを受け昭和37年、ついに梅酒が解禁され、昭和46年にはブドウ類を除く全面解禁にいたります。まさに果実酒維新でした。

自由を勝ち取ってから半世紀、あらゆる分野において手作り文化が衰退する中、果実酒も同じ様相を呈しています。この緊急事態に居ても立って

[Afterword]

Plum wine (umeshu), which was customarily made by farmers around the time when I was born, was, strictly speaking, a violation of the Liquor Tax Law.

It was Minori Ishida who stood up to put a stop to this sad reality.

Mr. Ishida, who was a public relations advisor to the Cabinet, proudly praised plum wine in his articles for the Nihon Keizai Shimbun in 1961, argued against the Ministry of Finance and the National Tax Agency and drove them into a corner.

Backed by public opinion, the ban on plum wine was finally lifted in 1962, and in 1971, the ban on fruit liqueurs was lifted entirely except for grapes.

This was truly a fruit liqueur restoration.

Half a century after winning the freedom for fruit liqueurs, while handmade culture is declining in a whole host of fields, fruit liqueur is also suffering the same fate.

I couldn't just sit still and do nothing during the state of emergency, and so I decided to stand up as an ambassador of fruit liquor based on my knowledge and experience.

My life with handmade fruit liquors started with a fascination with plum wine and has now come full circle after spells with a variety of handmade liqueurs, wild grass liqueurs,

もいられず、わずかな知識と経験をもとに果実酒伝道師として立ち上がりました。

梅酒に魅了され、果実酒・野草酒・薬膳酒・漢方薬酒など、あまたの手作り酒を経て果実酒に戻ってきた私の手作り果実酒人生。果実酒をいかにしたら復興できるかが、私に残された人生の課題です。

豊かな日本の季節感を表現する二十四節気や、海外から入ってきた新しいイベントと果実酒をコラボさせたらどうか？英語を入れて外国の人達にも日本文化としての手作り果実酒を知ってほしい。

これらを表現する方法を模索していた中で、中之条ビエンナーレでの星野博美さんとの出会いがありました。懐かしくも新しい表現のイラストや切り絵に魅了されて制作依頼、手作り果実酒レシ

medicinal liqueurs, and Chinese herbal liqueurs.

How to make it so fruit liqueurs prosper again is a challenge I will dedicate the rest of my life to.

I thought to myself 'why don't I do some kind of collaboration between fruit liqueurs and the 24 solar terms (24 sekki) that express the rich seasonal senses of Japan, or the new events that have been introduced from overseas?'

I want people from overseas to learn about handmade fruit liqueurs as a part of Japanese culture by teaching about them in English.

While searching for a way to express this idea, I met Hiromi Hoshino at the Nakanojo Biennale.

I was fascinated by the nostalgic and yet novel expression of her illustrations and collages and I asked her to work on the production, which came to fruition as an illustrated book of handmade fruit liqueur recipes.

The title is 'Fruits Wine Calendar', and I think many felt uncomfortable with the decision to name it this.

I also thought that handmade fruit liqueur, which is seen as a mixed liqueur in Japan,

ピ絵本として結実したのです。

　なお、表題が『Fruit Wine Calendar』とな
っており、違和感を覚える方も多いと思います。
日本的には混成酒である手作り果実酒は『Fruit
Liqueur』と呼ぶべきと私も思っていました。ただ、
梅酒は海外でプラムワインと言われることも多い
ということで、その表現を拝借させていただいた
次第です。

　出版に当たっては多くの方々にお力添えをいた
だきました。特に共同出版という形でご承諾いた
だいた星野博美さん、上毛新聞社・出版部の一倉
基益様、ベースになる果実酒レシピの考案を後押
して発表の企画「よいしれ六合」を主催してくれ
た古川葉子さん、英語翻訳を快諾いただきました
唐沢トランスレーションの唐澤浩一様、クラウド
ファンディング会社・Readyforの皆様には大変お

should be called 'Fruits Liqueur' and not 'Fruits Wine'.

However, as umeshu is often referred to as plum wine overseas, I decided to keep it consistent with the expression of plum wine.

Many people helped in getting the book published.

In particular, I would like to say a big thank you to Ms. Hiromi Hoshino, who agreed to publish the book as a joint effort; Mr. Motoeki Ichikura of the publishing department at Jomo Shimbun; Ms. Yoko Furukawa, who supported the idea of a book based on fruit liqueur recipes and hosted the event, 'Yoishire Kuni', to announce the project; Mr. Koichi Karasawa of Karasawa Translation Service for kindly agreeing to translate the book into English, and everyone at the crowdfunding company Readyfor.

世話になりました。そして、私のわがままを支え、叱咤激励してきた糟糠の妻？早子にも深く深く感謝しています。さらに、ご支援・ご助言・ご協力をいただきました全ての方々にこの場を借りて心より感謝申し上げます。

此度の自費出版に当たりましては、資金不足を補うべく63歳にして初体験のクラウドファンディングを敢行し、多くの方々にご支援をいただきました。この本は皆さまのおかげで形になり生まれる事ができました。ここにお名前を掲載し、感謝の言葉に代えさせていただきます。なお、一部お名前掲載を希望されなかった方々にも謹んでお礼申し上げます。

ありがとう・ありがとう・ありがとうございました！！

Lastly, I would like to say a huge thank you to my wife Hayako who has allowed me to follow my dream and spurred me on to complete the book.

I would also like to take this opportunity to express my sincere thanks to all those who have supported, advised, or helped in the making of this book.

For this self-publishing effort, I engaged in crowdfunding for the first time at the age of 63 to make up for the lack of funds, and as a result, this book received support from many people.

Thanks to all of you, this book was able to take shape and be published.

I would like to thank the following people.

I would also like to express my sincere gratitude to those who did not wish to have their names included.

A big thank you to you all!

【主な参考文献】

◆日本の七十二候を楽しむ　文：白井明大　絵：有賀一広／東邦出版

◆暮らしのならわし十二か月　文：白井明大　絵：有賀一広／飛鳥新社

◆原色牧野和漢薬草大圖鑑／北隆館

◆食材図典／小学館

◆未病を治す　薬膳酒　渡邉修著　薬日本堂監修／法研

◆香りと花のハーブ図鑑500／主婦の友社

◆木の酒・草の酒・果実の酒　石田穰　清水大典著／家の光協会

◆果実酒・薬酒　作り方楽しみ方　清水大典　安藤博著／家の光協会

◆ハーブ大百科　デニ・バウン著　吉村則子・石原真理訳／誠文堂新光社

◆こよみを使って年中行事を楽しむ本　2017／神宮館

◆ウィキペディア

[Main References]

◆ Nihon-no-Shichijuniko-wo-Tanoshimu (Enjoy the 72 Pentads of Japan) Written by: Akehiro Shirai, Illustrations by: Kazuhiro Aruga / Toho Publishing

◆ Kurashi-no-Narawashi Ju Ni-Kagetsu (Twelve Months of Living Customs) Written by: Akehiro Shirai Illustrations by: Kazuhiro Aruga / Asukashinsha

◆ Illustrated Medicinal Plants of the World in Color / Hokuryukan

◆ Shokuzai Zuten (Food's Food) / Shogakukan

◆ Mibyo-wo-Naosu Yakuzenshu (Curing Ill Health before Symptoms Occur) Written by: Osamu Watanabe, Supervising editor:　NIHONDO / Houken

◆ Kaori-to-Hana-no-Habu Zukan (Illustrated Book of 500 Fragrances and Flowering Herbs) SHUFUNOTOMO

◆ Ki-no-Sake Kusa-no-Sake Kajitsu-no-Sake (Wood Liqueurs, Herb Liqueurs, Fruit Liqueurs) Written by: Minori Ishida, Daisuke Shimizu / IE-NO-HIKARI Association

◆ Kajitsushu & Yakushu Tsukurikata-Tanoshimikata (How to Make & Enjoy Fruit and Medicinal Liquors) Written by: Daisuke Shimizu and Hiroshi Ando / IE-NO-HIKARI Association

◆ Habu Daihyakka (Encyclopedia of Herbs & Their Uses) Written by: Deni Bown, Translated by Noriko Yoshimura and Mari Ishihara / Seibundo Shinkosha Publishing

◆ Koyomi-wo-Tsukatte Nendjugyoji-wo-Tanoshimu Hon 2017 (Book to Enjoy the Yearly Events with Koyomi, 2017) / Jingukan

◆ Wikipedia

著者 渡邉 修 （わたなべ おさむ）

薬酒果実酒伝道師。
茨城大学農芸化学科卒業。
大手食品メーカーの商品開発として15年勤務の後、手作り
の薬酒果実酒を提供する店を開業。
その後、薬草公園（薬王園）がある群馬県中之条町に移住。
薬酒果実酒歴は50年を超え、おいしい果実酒を広めるため
の活動をライフワークとして、出版や講習会等の啓蒙活動を
続けている。
1957年生まれ。群馬県高崎市出身。
著書に『元気酒』（家の光協会）、『未病を治す　薬膳酒』（法研）。
『薬膳酒』は『養生酒』の書名で台湾・中国でも現地出版される。

Author Osamu Watanabe

Osamu Watanabe is an ambassador for medicinal and
fruit liqueurs.
He graduated from the Department of Agricultural
Chemistry, Ibaraki University.
After working for 15 years in product development at a
major food manufacturer, he opened a store that offered
handmade medicinal liqueurs and fruit liqueurs.
He then moved to Nakanojo Town in Gunma Prefecture,
where the herb garden Yakuoen is located.
With over 50 years of experience in medicinal liqueurs
and fruit liqueurs, he continues to carry out educational
activities such as publishing books and conducting
seminars as his lifework to promote delicious fruit
liqueurs.
He was born in 1957 in Takasaki City, Gunma Prefecture.
His books include 'Genki Sake' (IE-NO-HIKARI
Association) and 'Yakuzenshu: Curing Ill Health before
Symptoms Occur' (Houken).
'Yakuzenshu' is also published locally in Taiwan and
China under the name 'Yǎngshēng Jiǔ'.

イラスト 星野 博美 (ほしの　ひろみ)

多摩美術大学造形表現学部絵画科卒業。
地域型芸術祭 中之条ビエンナーレへの関わりを機に、2009
年から群馬県中之条町に移住。現在　農家で働きながら、里
山の暮らしのなかで収穫したイメージをもとに制作活動を続
けている。
1978年生まれ。愛知県出身。

Illustrations by Hiromi Hoshino

Hiromi Hoshino graduated from the Faculty of Fine
arts,Tama Art University.
She moved to Nakanojo Town in Gunma prefecture
in 2009 upon being involved in a regional art festival
'Nakanojo Biennale'.
Working with farmers,and living at satoyama area.
She continues art works inspired by 'local' landscapes
and people.
Born in 1978,and is from Aichi Prefecture.

ご支援くださった皆様

梶澤　勇人	関口　文彦	akanene
モッチーママ	イナリヤト食文化研究所	富澤　渉
松本　博明	ジュリアーノナカニシ	福田　公雄
岡安　賢一	たいらせいこ	西島　雄志
武智伊知郎	星野　陽子	藤山　周平
たろ＆もも	Miho Nishikata	藤山　倫子
桑本のり子	神部美佐子	藤山生来雲
鈴木　禎子	nakanojyo kraft project	齋木　利一
S&B 本栖天狗	大和　由佳	古賀あかね
齋藤　典子	ふじなみ	唐沢トランスレーションサービス
沢渡温泉 三喜屋旅館	伊東　憲正	菅川　雅晴
ハーブおじさん	石原　節子	竹澤　結花
長井　斎	㈱桃ケ丘リトルプレイス	TOKIフーズシステム
前田　隆	江黒　孝夫	森のハープ弾き 阿久津瞳
橋本　桂子	淀　昌宏	山口農園
小嶋　嘉子	三友　昭彦	M.Iriuchi
古川　葉子	永井多津也	西村　欣也
恐竜のお母ちゃん	yotacco	西川　健
末吉　英一	吉田　和典	よしだ農園
曽根原詠子	佐藤　美和	水野　暁
菅　典子	松永　洋子	里山未来舎 渡陽平（わたりん）
諸角　容子	フラーやよい	寺西　らら
八戸せんべい	箱田みどり	浅野　桃子
小林　朋寛	齋木　三男	中嶋　栄
SUNATA	にし ゆみこ	CLEMOMO
金子　敦子	ハイジ	三川　貴也
Junko H.	本木　陽一	Maebashi Art Walk
Miwako	村田　春子	茂木保奈美
中西　友	YORIKO	武井　仁美
石井　資子	宮崎亜由美	森川　和光
Junko K.	飯沢　康輔	西田　真実
原沢　香司	狩野　初美	Naka
くらしの宿Cocoro	山口　惠子	
かま猫	原沢　恵子	

（お名前は順不同、敬称は略させていただきました。）

果実酒歳時記
～季節を味わう果実酒暮らし～

2021年5月8日発行　初版一刷
2021年12月1日発行　初版二刷

文　渡邉 修

絵　星野 博美

発行　上毛新聞社出版部
〒371-8666　前橋市古市町1−50−21
TEL 027−254−9966
FAX 027−254−9965
✉ book@raijin.com

禁無断転載・複製
落丁・乱丁本は送料小社負担にてお取り替え
いたします。